D1083864

THE
BLUE COLLAR CEO

THE BLUE COLLAR CEO

My Gutsy Journey from Rookie
Contractor to Multi-Millionaire
Construction Boss

MANDY RENNEHAN

Collins

The Blue Collar CEO
Copyright © 2022 by Mandy Rennehan.
All rights reserved.

Published by Collins, an imprint of HarperCollins Publishers Ltd

First edition

Blue Collar CEO® is a trademark owned by Freshco Retail Maintenance.

No part of this book may be used or reproduced in any manner
whatsoever without the prior written permission of the publisher,
except in the case of brief quotations embodied in reviews.

HarperCollins books may be purchased for educational, business,
or sales promotional use through our Special Markets Department.

HarperCollins Publishers Ltd
Bay Adelaide Centre, East Tower
22 Adelaide Street West, 41st Floor
Toronto, Ontario, Canada
M5H 4E3

www.harpercollins.ca

Library and Archives Canada Cataloguing in Publication

Title: The blue collar CEO : my gutsy journey from rookie contractor to multi-millionaire
construction boss / Mandy Rennehan.
Names: Rennehan, Mandy, author.
Identifiers: Canadiana (print) 20220135010 | Canadiana (ebook) 20220135037 | ISBN
9781443461931 (hardcover) | ISBN 9781443461948 (ebook)
Subjects: LCSH: Rennehan, Mandy. | LCSH: Women chief executive officers—Canada—
Biography. | LCSH: Businesswomen—Canada—Biography. | LCSH: Construction
industry—Canada. | LCGFT: Autobiographies.
Classification: LCC HD9715.C32 R46 2022 | DDC ON ORDER NOV 2021 |
338.4/7624092—dc23

Printed and bound in the United States of America

LSC/H 10 9 8 7 6 5 4 3 2 1

To my bro and best buddy. It's bullshit we have had to
continue without you and your stinky-ass feet. "Missing you"
is an understatement—it doesn't even come close.

CONTENTS

THE
BLUE
COLLAR
CEO

PROLOGUE

—

SUCCESS = MA ON HER MOWER

Ma had just turned seventy. She took a zero turn, quick and smooth, on the John Deere commercial mower I'd sprung for. It was another beautiful July day in seaside Nova Scotia, where Ma spends half her time mowing the lawn of my 18-acre compound in Yarmouth—with its blow-your-mind views of the Bay of Fundy—and the other half willing the grass to grow. Faster. She loves the mowing that much. We call that machine her later-in-life best friend.

There she was, in her happy place, absorbed in cutting those even rows. She had no idea I was there.

I waited for her to finish a long stretch, then crept up behind her on my buggy. I got right up close. She pulled another sharp turn and found herself facing me, head on.

"Mandy Dawn!" she screeched.

She wanted to mow me over. Just this once. I could tell. But instead, with a big saucy grin, she bounced around me and drove off to finish the row.

The sun was high on that hill. Her skin was bright pink. I yelled, "Ma, you look like a lobster in a pot that somebody forgot about!"

She idled the machine, looked back at me through her grass-covered glasses, her fifteen-year-old Blue Jays World Series hat askew atop her head, and said, "You listen here, Mandy! You mind your business and leave me and my boyfriend here, John Deere, alone."

I roared laughing. She zipped off. A bit of my heart—a happy, contented, grateful bit—went with her.

Not three minutes later, I heard another motor. It was Pup, my dad, making his way up the long driveway, riding side saddle at 65 kilometres an hour on our property's four-wheeler, the landscape cart in tow. Yes, side saddle. And as full of himself as the rooster that got you out of bed at 5 a.m.

Had anyone asked me when I was young what my markers for success would be, I doubt seeing my mother on a tractor or Pup zooming by on a four-wheeler would have topped the list. But when I talk to young people and they ask me what's best about growing older, I say to them, "Who the hell doesn't want to be a millionaire?" The kids' teachers will tell me no one's quite taken that approach before. But I frame it for them this way: it's not about the money; it's not about getting rich. It's that maybe, someday, you could send your parents on a trip they couldn't otherwise afford. You could buy someone you love, who's struggling, something they need. I make it about giving. One of the kids will say, "Yeah, I could buy my parents a new house." And I tell them that's just what I did when I became a millionaire: I bought my mom and dad a house.

Now, my folks don't live together on that big seaside acreage anymore. They're no longer married. But they both take care of it—they've even found a kind of peace with each other in the project. They're remarkably able to put their differences aside to work on the windmill property. (Keep your pants on. I'll tell you all about the windmill later.)

The truth is, my mission, from as far back as I can remember, has been to make my parents' lives easier. Mowing that acreage brings out a joy and assertiveness in Ma, a real contentment that I never saw enough of growing up. Building a multi-million-dollar business, as a female and as a lesbian, in an industry that still, three decades into my career, barely knows what to do with either, has been hard, to say the least. You wouldn't credit how hard. Some people go through life in the left lane of a busy freeway without a speed limit or off-ramps. So much for the lucky few. The rest of us find ourselves on dirt roads full of potholes and deep ditches.

At times, I've wondered if I was on a road at all.

But has it been worth it?

Show me Ma, fierce and proud, whipping around out there on her tractor. Give me a glimpse of Pup zipping past on the four-wheeler, happy as a clam. Then ask me that question again.

1

STAPLE YOUR HEMS AND FACE THE PIPER

What's your first move when you really don't know what to do next? You call your Newfoundland friend.

She answered on the first ring, as if she could feel the urgency.

San Francisco, I told her. The Paris of North America. The Golden Gate Bridge.

Most importantly, though, I told her this: the Gap had come calling. I laid out the opportunity in my best "this is the real deal" voice. I needed her to understand how bloody serious this was. There are things you'll never have a second chance at. This trip would be my ticket, the genesis of my actual career, the one I'd been building toward.

Or it wouldn't.

My life was about to change, one way or the other.

I was twenty-four years old, an entrepreneur from small-town Nova Scotia on her way up. Way up. Sprung, in all my unlikely splendour, straight out of Canada's Maritimes. And I wasn't just some ordinary businesswoman to contend with. I was a one-woman revolution in the making, a visionary, kickass lesbian in the trades—a lesbian *rethinking* the trades, the whole goddamn construction industry, thank you very much.

Of course the Gap had come calling. I know, right?

Underneath that, though, I was a lobster fisherman's daughter who'd started out catching bait in the Bay of Fundy. I'd worked for years as a farmhand, feeding and—I'm not kidding you—herding cows on local farms. I'd spent what seemed (to me) like a lifetime of night shifts mopping layers of beer and puke off the floors of Halifax pubs. San Francisco? The Gap? Seriously? I'd never set foot on the US West Coast. Shit, I'd turned twenty-one before I'd eaten my first garden salad. Now I was about to fly cross-continent to make a pitch to take over facilities maintenance for every one of this retail giant's 230-plus Canadian stores.

Holy check-your-pants shit.

Midway through my spiel to my friend, I heard a commotion in the background.

"Okay," I said. "What the hell are you doing?"

"Jeez, b'y! I'm packing my shit and coming on that plane with you!"

For anyone unlucky enough to have never set foot on The Rock on Canada's East Coast, "b'y" is Newfoundland English for "boy," which, further, is Newfoundland English for "buddy" or "friend." An outsider needs a sharp ear—and maybe a translator—to make their way in that glorious salt-caked land.

Newfoundland wasn't asking. She was telling. And it sounded like she was throwing everything she owned, plus her Aunt Lucy besides, into her suitcase.

I haven't come across many people who could make me laugh

more easily than Newfoundland. She was the sort who held nothing back. You never had to wonder what she was thinking. That's my kind of person. Real.

She flew into Halifax to meet me. We had a few hours before the flight to California. Once there, we'd head straight from the airport to Gap's headquarters. But as she approached me out of her arrivals gate, she looked me up and down and said, "Yeah, you're not going into that meeting with those clothes on, my friend."

I was in jeans (ripped), work boots, and a hoodie. Job site clothes. Okay, *my* clothes. Period. My hair was pulled back, but not with flair—just to get it the hell out of my face.

Newfoundland shook her head. "You've got to look respectable."

The next thing you know, we were zipping through the city and pulling up to a Reitmans store. That's right, Reitmans. Where else could I get the female corporate look on a shoestring budget? I have always hated shopping, and I detest trying on clothes. It just feels like a waste of time: there's always something else I could be doing. But I trusted her intentions. I sucked it up. My friend pushed me around that store like she was on a mission. She picked out the most professional-looking shirt and pants she could find—and got me into them. The pants were a bit long, but they'd do. I walked up to the cash fully clad in my new duds and paid for what I was wearing. We ripped the tags off and headed back to the airport.

I should have spent my time on that long flight focusing on the meeting, but, dammit, the breath coming off the guy next to me could have peeled the carpet off the floor. And I was too nervous to eat a full meal. By the time the plane landed, I was full of peanuts and cheap coffee—and swearing I would never again, as long as I lived, let anyone book me into a middle seat on an airplane. (I have

7

kept that promise.) We caught a cab to the company's building near the waterfront, a stunning modern structure with chunky cube-style layers and echoes of old warehouses in its design: brick walls filled with rows of vast grilled windows. We stood outside and stared, then looked at each other and broke out into great big, nervous grins.

I was in San Francisco, about to meet with senior executives representing what was, at that time, the biggest retailer in the world.

This was happening.

Suddenly, I was sweating like Trump trying to form a sentence. I had never done anything like this before. However, by this point new territory was a daily occurrence for me. My young company was growing, fast: I was doing a million dollars' worth of business a year, including, already, the maintenance for forty of Gap's Canadian locations. If I landed this contract my company's annual takings would leap—overnight—to five million dollars. Didn't the Great One, Gretzky, tell us you miss a hundred percent of the shots you don't take? I knew my shit. That was why I was here. I had one shot. And I was aiming for the net.

We made our way inside. The place was hopping with people rushing back and forth. This young guy armed with a headset and a clipboard hurried down the hallway to get us.

"Hey, Canada," he said. "We're running behind. You've got seven minutes."

Then he turned and walked away.

Newfoundland looked at me and blurted, "What a dick!" Inside, I agreed with her. He was totally dickish. We're East Coasters, after all. We're all about making people feel welcome. If the tables had been turned, Mr. Pressed Khakis would have been presented with a cold craft beer and a lobster sandwich, with a few East Coast jokes thrown in for good measure.

But holy shit. There were all these people around, and her voice carried—way more loudly than I was comfortable with. I had to shush her. "You can't say that here!"

I shook off my irritation. Had to. It was game time. I walked toward those double doors like I was the one who'd actually called the meeting.

"Holy crap, Bear. Stop!"

I swung around. Newfoundland said in a harsh whisper, "Lord thundering Jesus, both hems fell out of your pants. You can't go in like that!"

It was a classic case of you get what you pay for. I must have stepped on them while I was sitting down, or getting up—remember how they were too long?—and snagged the hems. I was uncomfortable in those clothes as it was. My feet, stuffed into these smart little shoes we'd bought, were killing me. Newfoundland sent me to the washroom. As I turned, I saw her spin sideways and dive into a nearby office. My seven minutes were racing by. I told myself to breathe. I'd barely finished the thought when she joined me—with a smile, and a loaded weapon.

A stapler.

I had no words. But Newfoundland, bent over and fumbling with the bottoms of my pants, sure did. "Holy shit, b'y, you've got to jump up on the counter so I can see what I'm doing."

I hopped up and sat. Right smack in a pool of water. The woman before me must have had a serious hot flash. There was water everywhere. I imagined her standing there in a mad panic, splashing water all over, trying to cool herself off. Thank God my pants were black, because my arse was soaked.

Newfoundland and I started to laugh.

But the clock was ticking. She got to work with the stapler. Thirty seconds later, my pants were "hemmed." Then she had me back up against the hand dryer—the shitty kind they had in those days, that would barely ruffle the hair on a mosquito's head. We grabbed wads of those useless, stiff paper towels you once found in every public washroom, and she had her hands all over my arse, trying to soak up the water.

My seven minutes had turned to four. I gave Newfoundland a look that was probably half-deranged. "I have to get in there."

She looked me square in the face and said, "You got this."

Back in the hallway she nodded in the direction of Mr. Khaki Pants. She knew what I was thinking. She leaned in and whispered, "Don't worry about him. If he tries to go near that door before you're finished, I'll take his headphones and ram them up his—"

I didn't hear the rest, because I was walking toward the meeting room: me and my stapled pants and my sopping wet butt and my Canadian East Coast personality.

When those giant doors opened, it was as dramatic as the parting of the Red Sea. The first person I saw was the big guy, Francisco, the Gap's senior vice-president of sourcing and procurement. He stood, and I looked up. I wouldn't be far off if I said I stood a groundhog above his belly button. That's how tall he was. The pinching dress shoes that I'd quickly come to hate added next to nothing to my short stature.

He smiled. "Hi, Mandy Rennehan. How are you?"

I shook his hand and then made my way around the room, shaking more hands. The boardroom table, at least 25 feet long, was made of some exotic, flawless wood and was surrounded by high-backed leather chairs that clearly didn't come from Staples (no offence intended). The view from the room's massive windows took in the Oakland Bay Bridge. I was briefly rattled by the thought of how much this view must cost. Then I turned my attention to the business at hand.

I faced a group of men, five of them. They looked perfectly at home around that pricy table. Professional. Intimidating. And yet, something in me said, "I'll have ya warmed up in no time, boys."

Francisco smiled at me. "You come very, very highly recommended," he began. "I'm interested in what you have to say."

I swallowed hard. I remembered the promise I'd made to myself: to always be me, the real Mandy. I would never try to be the person I thought they were expecting.

"Well, it's a good thing," I said, with what I hoped was my most winning smile. "Because, you know what? Canadian lesbians don't travel to San Francisco all dressed up like this for just any guys."

Dead silence. The five men stared at me. Their faces didn't crack for the longest three seconds of my life.

The key to a great lobster catch comes in the form of a little fish that travels upstream with lots and lots of friends. That tiny creature lives at sea but spawns in fresh water. In the bustling metropolis of Yarmouth, Nova Scotia, where I grew up—population just 8,500, but it's a community that boasts Atlantic Canada's biggest and most diverse fishery—we call this little fish a "kayak." It's also known as a gaspereau or an alewife. But no matter what you call them, they're akin to a five-star Michelin meal to our precious crustaceans, drawing them in like an East Coaster to a fried baloney sandwich on squishy white bread.

As a kid, I was keenly aware of the importance of this little fish to the well-being of our family.

There's nothing quite like growing up as the daughter of a lobster fisherman in a family of six in a community that relies heavily on the seasonal, unreliable fishing industry. In the late 1970s and early 1980s of my childhood, lobster was the furthest thing from a so-called delicacy. It was known as "poor man's food." And those who caught and sold it barely got by. In our household, we were always trying to beat our way through what life threw at us. Flared tempers were normal, worry was second nature, and anxiety came and went with the tides. Where was the next cheque coming from? How was the next bag of groceries going to make it to the table? Where would we find the money to put gas in the car? And let's not think about what would be under the Christmas tree—Christmas really was the time for miracles. We kids came to believe in them, because as far as we knew there was just no other way those gifts could have appeared beneath the tree.

Born in 1975 on a typical stormy day in Rockville, just down the rocky coastline from Yarmouth, I'm Mandy to Ma, Bear to friends, and Sis to my brothers and Pup. I showed up five years after my older brother Troy, and seven years after the eldest, Chris. I spent the nine months before I was born with my twin, Trev, living in a 1970s rendition of a cramped studio apartment with a belly button for a doorbell. I don't know what the hell went on in there, but beyond our later mutual love for Ma's jam-in-the-middle sugar cookies (and thick-ass egg sandwiches on squishy white bread), we came out so polar opposite that you'd never guess we were twins.

We don't look alike. We don't have the same personality. Trev always loved watching sports and placing bets with the boys. I, on the other hand, couldn't tell you who was playing what sport on television because I was on the field or court playing the sports myself. While Trev was memorizing the *Wheel of Fortune* answers on his Xbox so his buddies would think he was smarter than they were, I was dreaming of a life outside of Yarmouth.

My twin was quiet as quiet could be. I was boisterous and full of questions.

We've all experienced someone like me in our lives—that kid who asks "why" and keeps asking "why" with every answer. My hunger for knowledge was insatiable. Why do cows get milked in the morning? Why does hay have to be bailed? Why do lobsters love to eat kayaks? The "how" questions were even more unending, because I just had to know how to do everything that needed doing.

I was lucky no one shooed me away. The adults, God bless them, just kept answering my questions. Or trying to. My parents did their best, after all. They never put up barriers for me. And there was never so much as the tiniest hint or suggestion that I take any of our hardships on myself. Home was a safe place: three meals a day, a bed to sleep in, and a side order of brothers to torment the shit out of me. But the struggles we lived through as a family drove me to strive for a different life. What I lacked was a mentor. Who was I going to learn from? Mentorship in my day consisted of Pup or Ma pointing at the door and hollering, "Get yer arse outside and get the stink blown off ya! Supper will be ready at 5."

Talk about Resilience-Building 101.

Okay, so I had no mentor. But I had myself. My own take on life. Which was definitely—how do I put this?—not quite what everyone expected when I was born: me, the first and only girl in the whole extended family, on both sides. When I showed up there was so much excitement I was practically smothered in bows and frills. Everyone invested in pink. Little did they know.

I was a tomboy from the very beginning. For me, wearing a dress was akin to Superman wearing a pair of kryptonite socks. *Get it off me!* Obviously there was more to this than just tomboy tendencies, but no one, least of all me, knew it.

Everything in its time.

Meanwhile, I had ideas. I had plans. I was never embarrassed when

I couldn't do something the first time. I'd keep at a task until I had it mastered. (Did I mention I came out breech? Ma has never let me forget it.) I had a bottomless need to make things better. By the age of ten, I may not have been able to articulate it, but the entrepreneur in me was jumping up and down, waving her arms, begging me to give her the attention she deserved. Watching Pup relentlessly working at fishing until he fought to keep his eyes open, could barely put one foot in front of the other—that had awakened a sleeping giant in me. My ambition was peskier than a blackfly looking for a snack at bedtime. I knew I had to find a way to help.

It didn't take me long to figure out what to do. It called for kayaks. Lots and lots of kayaks.

It's not that I wasn't a kid who loved to do kid stuff—I was, and I did—but while other kids were busy with Red Rover, Red Rover, I started building real-life teams. While they were fishing in the creek for something to do, I cast my net in the river to see a profit.

The plan was simple and brash. I had two things going for me: personality and athletic ability. There wasn't a sport I couldn't play, and the boys all wanted me on their teams. I always got picked first, because I was better than they were. So I rounded up four local guys and told them, "I'll be your winger for the hockey game this weekend, but you gotta dip kayaks with me."

Sold. It was a done deal, just like that. Bargaining rule number one: never downplay your assets and talents.

We had to wait for low tide, when the fish were swimming upstream. Tides are always shifting, and, around the time of our scheme, the lowest tide was pretty late, around 10 p.m. I don't know what tricks the boys used for sneaking out. I manoeuvred around our home's squeaky floorboards the way the Road Runner skirted Acme bombs. *Beep, beep!* The idea was to escape unseen so we wouldn't have to shift to Plan B, which was to run like hell so our arses wouldn't get whooped.

We made our own dip nets with bent wood instead of steal. We'd tie the wood into a circle, install hooks for the bait bags, and fasten them to long arms we could extend over the wide Chegoggin River. The kayaks struggling heroically upstream swim right in, and you haul your catch back to shore. In some places, the water was shallow enough that you could wade out a little way. Our favourite spot was down from Cranberry Hill, just upriver from a group of my brothers' friends, older kids who were always complaining about having to do the work. Nothing burns my arse more than lazy people. So I figured we should get to the kayaks first. They were welcome to the ones that escaped our nets—the leftovers.

The boys and I would load our catches into feed bags. Somehow, we had to get those heavy bags up my driveway, then load them on the truck. The problem was the hill we had to climb. So I borrowed a set of training wheels off the bike of a kid who lived down the street and put them on my own bike. The wheels made my bike more stable to ride with a heavy load. I'd pedal the bags up the hill and heap everything onto the truck before Pup got up at 3:30 in the morning to head down to the wharf.

I remember Pup asking me one day, "Mandy, why in the love of hell do you have training wheels on your bike?"

"Because I think it's funny," I replied, turning around so he couldn't read my face.

Pup's boss loved him for showing up to work with all that bait. And I loved that he looked good and didn't have to catch the kayaks himself. He always gave credit where it was due (or where he *thought* it was due), so he would bring the cash back and tell me, "Hey, sweetie, give the money to the guys on the street and tell them keep up the good work."

"Yep, whatever you say, Pup." Fingers crossed behind my back. He didn't have a level clue that I was the actual "fish-bait broker," and he didn't need to know. I cut the guys in at 10 percent. Fair is fair, after all, but it meant more to them that they got to pick me first for the next game.

Me? This little Bear stashed away every single penny she could. I set some aside to get Ma a gift certificate at the Cut & Curl in town and some to put toward the new scope I knew Pup wanted for rabbit hunting. Things I'd hear them talk about that they wished they could afford.

As for the rest, I knew exactly what I was going to spend my own savings on.

All secrets come out in the end. One creaky floorboard and—uh oh, was I in for it. No one could do a proper tongue lashing quite like Pup.

"Mandy. What the hell are you doing leaving the house this time of night? It's 10 o'clock girl!"

Breathe. Show no fear. "Well, I wanna go dip kayaks, Pup." Calm as can be.

"Oh no you're not!" He pointed that calloused finger toward my bedroom.

Okay, fine. Time for Operation Escape: slide window up softly, leg over the sill, roll body over and onto the grass outside, and land with a thud. Not a pretty sight. Then run for your life down the hill.

I knew full well he'd probably kick my arse into next week for disobeying, but I also knew how important it was that those bait bags were on his truck when he headed out in a few hours. There was work to be done.

It turns out that this particular night would be life changing. The kayaks were running so fast and so plentiful, the boys and I couldn't keep up. I knew that, to really help my family, to make more money than I'd ever seen at one time in my life, we'd need backup. That meant owning up to my nightly escapades, consequences be damned. I had no choice. I tore up the hill on that bike as if my life depended on it. I didn't even feel the burn.

I'm not sure what sold Pup and my brothers. Maybe it was the look on my face, or desperation in my voice. Whatever did it, they were in, and we all hauled ass back to the river. We caught thirty bags of fish that night, compared with a regular night's three or four. Instead of the usual twelve or thirteen dollars the boys and I would split between us, those thirty bags made us—well, you do the math. To me, it added up to a fortune. We all worked together: Pup, me, my brothers, and the neighbourhood boys, hauling in that massive catch. I still remember how good that felt.

Well, it felt good for about a minute. Job finished, it was time to face the piper. A "discussion" took place. When all was said and done, and Pup realized who the real fish broker was, he just stared at me. He. Just. Stared.

I stood completely still.

He finally stammered out, "What in the love of—? Who the hell are you? You're ten!"

Pup still looks at me the same way when I surprise him. I call it "the infamous Pup glare."

I've looked back on that night many, many times. It serves as a reminder that if we don't take chances, we miss our greatest opportunities. The fish broker business was a means to an end. I knew that no type of fishing would be in my future, but that didn't mean I wouldn't take advantage of what it had to offer. Scared? Hell, yes. That shit—fear—doesn't go away. It hit me just as intensely all those years later, in San Francisco.

As I stood in that boardroom—staples, wet pants, and all—with the eyes of several Gap executives boring into me, nobody saying a word, a familiar feeling came over me. Fear? Absolutely, you bet. But something else, too. I felt just the way I'd felt at ten, the first time I found myself caught in the path of Pup's glare. It was an expression of shock and confusion, with maybe a hint of fury. It said, "Is this girl for real?" But it also said, "Yup, she's mine. And I'm proud of her."

In other words, I felt hope.

2

A GIRL LIKE YOU NEEDS A HAMMER (AND A PLAN ... AND A TEAM)

My first real hammer was a thing of beauty.

It was the first tool I bought with my own money. Fish broker profits tucked in my pocket, I hopped a ride into town and headed for Home Hardware on Main Street. I made a beeline for the tool section. A kid in a candy store had nothing on me. I took my time, and when I was satisfied with my choice, I walked up to the checkout as proud as could be.

The guy at the counter looked at me with a smile and said, "What does a young thing like you need a hammer for? You gonna beat someone up?"

I'm sure he thought he was being funny. But I thought, *Keep it up, you nincompoop. You're just another dimwit who doesn't believe young females should be taken seriously.*

Hope you like the taste of my dust.

———

When I was knee-high to the chip drawer, my mother, Diane Mary Swim-Rennehan, was living life as a product of her time. You know the story: find a man, get married, pop out a couple of kids, do the housework, grin and bear the "ugly" life throws at you, then put all of this on repeat.

Years later I realized that, despite Ma's circumstances, the infectious permanent smile she wore when people were around (whether or not she liked these people) was a reflection of her down-home kindness and her ability to put her circumstances aside so she could focus on others. Ma is simply good to the bone.

Life wasn't easy for her, though. She carried with her a measure of shyness and a heaping helping of regret for having married my father without ever having had the confidence to stand up and ask, "Why don't we wait a while before we say 'I do'?" One simply didn't do such things in the era when man was king and the ultimate housewife was the expected calling for the half of the species who had breasts (and less facial hair).

It wasn't just my ma. Women weren't respected as workers, or as equals in general. Ideas about what a woman might want to "do" with her life were pooh-poohed. When I entered junior high, two mandatory courses popped up. One made me cringe and frustrated me no end: home economics. I hated home ec class with a passion. I had no patience for mixing, sifting, stirring, standing at a stove, all in an apron that I could never tie at the back. Today I appreciate the art of cooking. But back then, the whole enterprise was tarnished by the narrative around how females were supposed to be in the kitchen. Oh, and the apron.

The other mandatory course was industrial arts—a.k.a. shop. That was a different story. I'd gun her down to that class. Instructions like

"Here are your two pieces of metal—now weld them together" were music to my ears. I was in my element. I knew it wasn't, by society's standards, supposed to be my element. Luckily for me, I didn't care.

Women have made some great headway since then. Career people today who are on maternity leave and are making a difference in their respected professions are able to say, "I love that kid I just popped out. But holy shit. If you don't get me out of the house after six months, I'm gonna bust out!" These women have grown beyond the bowling-alley thinking that tells them there are only a certain number of pins they're going to knock down, and they don't have the option of getting a strike because, well, they're female.

But don't put away your shovel yet—there's still a lot more bullshit to toss out of the way. We still live in a world where some of our male counterparts prefer us amid a set of pretty Tupperware mixing bowls, with hand-embroidered aprons wrapped uncomfortably around our waists.

And that's why one of my questions to girls and young women is always: "What do you want to be when you grow up?"

For me, the answer to that question was never in doubt.

It's second nature to focus on what others think about us, and what they try to project on us. Mr. Home Hardware, who was trying to be funny with his comment, could have thrown me into an ugly tailspin of self-doubt. But I knew who I was, and I had a sense, even back then, of what I could accomplish. What other people thought of me, I decided, was none of my business.

Hammer, meet my other love: wood. You two will get along famously. As any artist chooses her medium, I chose oh-so-beautiful wood: whether sensually smooth or ruggedly rough; ironwood strong or soft, yielding pine; tough yet resilient; deeply exotic or simply natural; willingly moulded, planed, sanded, and stained to perfection, its rich grains rising to the surface. Did I mention you can run your hands over its silky smoothness? Mmm.

Folks, I tremble as I tell you what wood is to me. That's some sexy shit.

My love affair with construction started in childhood. Growing up rurally, surrounded by wooded areas, I developed a fascination for any tall-standing species that ended in "tree." Combine that with the fact that coming from a big family meant I craved an escape, and we had a match.

I'm not one to squander time with wishful thinking, hoping someone else will magically give me what I want. If I wanted a getaway, I'd have to build it myself. While other kids were busy building "forts" out of branches, my brain was in full-blown log cabin mode. The kind I saw pictures of in the magazines you'd flip through in the waiting room at the dentist's. They were basically logs, stacked, right? I was like, well, shit. I can do that.

After the success of the kayak venture, with my already semi-developed knack for business, I made my list of must-haves. They included a plan, a team, and some tools. One hammer, much as I loved it, wasn't going to cut it.

I'd become somewhat of a mini-expert in recruiting help. I'd learned how to motivate boys—but it certainly wasn't from using my body. Heck, I didn't even know I was gay at that point, but I've always known shaking what my mama gave me sure as hell wasn't a strategy I'd ever adopt. What I did know was, if you can get them out late at night to chase fish, recruiting for daytime assistance to build a super-cool fort should be a piece of cake.

It turned out I was right. All it cost me were a couple of hours of playing ball, which I loved to do anyway. I mean, who doesn't want to be part of constructing a fort on steroids? One log cabin coming up.

And what kind of entrepreneur would I be if I didn't always look for ways to save? There she stood: Grampy's shed, which stowed a collection of tools the likes of which I could only dream of owning. I used to watch Grampy sharpen them on the stone he kept on the counter. He had so many chisels and what-have-you that I knew I could probably get away with borrowing some of the older tools in the bottom of the box—he'd never even notice they were gone. But if I came right out and asked, he'd think it was ridiculous, me needing those tools. That I'd cut myself. That I was in over my head. No, I was better off to sneak in one day with a Foodland bag and walk back out with all the old, forgotten spare tools that, from watching him work, I thought we might need. I'd sharpen and clean them before putting them back. He'd never know.

With my own trusty hammer as the lead, we had everything we needed to get started. Except an axe. I had to make off with Pup's.

The learning curve was a story in itself. There we were, three or four kids in the woods, trying to cut down a tree with a dull axe. If you saw us it would have been like watching a small dog trying to hump a football. When we finally got one down, we had to shave it so it would stack properly and we wouldn't get snagged on the branches. That was even harder. And the boys weren't committed enough to stick around all day. They'd get a tree down and be like, "I'm outta here." So it came to this: they'd chop down the trees, which I would skin. There was sap everywhere, and we'd run out of trees in one spot and have to find another patch. But I was building up my arsenal of skills. I got to know that a birch tree was harder to cut down than, say, a spruce—which we have a ton of in Nova Scotia—but it could hold more weight without bending. And there was less sap. Pine trees were also soft, but they had a beautiful patina. I was on my way to understanding different types of wood and the pros and cons of each for construction.

When we finally managed to build a structure you could sit in, we ran logs vertically overtop and laid brush over that for the roof. I didn't understand trusses or how to cut them. When it rained, our brush roof would come right down on top of us. And we'd be like, Oh shit. We wanted a fort that would protect us from the elements.

So that was where my mind went next, and it never stopped going: to the next thing that needed learning, and the next. My love affair with construction had been sparked. Those structures still existed in the woods until 2014, when someone clearing a piece of land took them down. I figure they stood that long, even with their amateur engineering, because, well, they were #BearBuilt.

3

NEVER UNDERESTIMATE A HORSE— OR A DETOUR

decided, being the good daughter I was, that it was time to call home and check in with my mother.

"Dear, where are ya?" she asked.

"I'm gone, Ma."

I really was. Gone. Away from home. I was seventeen, and learning fast at a dairy farm on the outskirts of Halifax—and not just about farming. I'd shown up two weeks earlier with a stinky old Bauer hockey bag bursting with work clothes, a few "going out" clothes, and the contents of my secret drawer—nearly eighteen hundred dollars in hard-earned savings. Independence felt great. Not only was I herding and feeding more than fifty cows, cleaning their stalls, and setting them up on the milk machines twice a day, I'd also run headlong into my first lesbian love affair. My old life in Yarmouth—where I'd still been so confused about my attraction to women, I'd actually had a longtime boyfriend—was already blurring into a kind of dream.

On the phone, Ma showed no signs of any real concern. "Well, dear, what do you mean?"

She might have noticed I hadn't been around but, then, I seldom was: I'd often stayed at my boyfriend's place or with a friend. I'd sometimes go a week or more without coming home except to run in and grab some clean clothes. This time, though, I'd packed and partly cleaned out my room. My bed hadn't been slept in or touched.

"Ma, I moved away. I've been here for a couple of weeks."

"Okay, dear. Well, stay in touch."

That response is so East Coast. Nothing negative. No judgment. No dire concern, because she trusted me to make good decisions. How can I explain that our upbringing was so devoid of parental hovering that it hadn't even occurred to me to share my plans with my parents in advance? It's not that Ma didn't care—both my parents have always cared for and loved each of their children deeply. As long as we were safe, that's all that mattered. So I did just as my dear Ma asked. I stayed in touch.

I had no plans of becoming a farmer. Working for myself—someway, somehow—that was the ultimate goal. But meanwhile, farm work's what I was qualified for; it was my ticket out of Yarmouth and, I hoped, a means to start building my bank account. That I knew my way around a farm was no accident. It was by design—my own, going back several years.

Even in the rural Nova Scotia of my youth, where survival for so many depended on heading out on the water to fish, or on working the fields, there wasn't a hope in hell of dragging most teenagers out of bed early enough to dig worms or milk cows. And few had the mechanical wherewithal to figure out how to back up a hay cart by themselves.

Not many could match my amazing calf and thigh muscles—built up through sheer hard work—which allowed me to throw the hay more than four tiers high.

So, calls from local farmers looking for help came my way. This was after my bait-netting entrepreneurial success had become my next business venture: Mandy Rennehan, freelance farmhand.

Farming wasn't easy work, but in a who-shows-up-first contest with the sunrise, I usually came out the winner. With little sleep and tired muscles, I did the work efficiently and with a smile. I was creating my own version of Entrepreneurship and Innovation 101: find the gaps, fill them, and show the world who you are in the process. Regardless of the finer points of your personality, the person you want to show them is the one who always does the right thing, who's honest, and who gives their all to every task they take on.

Someone is always watching, and folks are always talking.

Folks like our East Coast farmers, a friendly bunch who have daily chinwags. My attitude and work ethic—so I was told—were often topics of discussion among them. I expect they were all a bit surprised that a short teenage girl could pull off the kind of physically demanding work they needed done.

But it wasn't just my determination and work ethic—or my strong legs—that made me a good bet. I'd learned my way around farm work long before I started making money at it.

The calf I planned to win the competition with was a beauty: mostly white, with a few veins of black and a round, brownish-purple circle right between her eyes. I named her "Plum," after my favourite fruit.

"Well, that's different," said our 4-H leader, Jordan, from behind his enormous red Lanny McDonald moustache. (Gosh, I love that drier-than-week-old-microwave-popcorn man.) Then he grinned. "Good luck, Renne."

I was the cool-kid athlete, but I was also in 4-H. My mouthier friends would say things like "Only nerds are in 4-H."

I'd shrug. "I guess I'm a nerd, then."

4-H is a highly respected global not-for-profit organization that focuses on character-building leadership skills and youth empowerment. To me, an eleven-year-old country bumpkin desperate to know not just how everything worked but how to do it all myself, 4-H was hands-on heaven. I learned how to milk a cow, plant seeds, and tend to crops. I learned all about the machinery it took to run a farm.

So what did I care if my friends, or anyone else, thought 4-H was for nerds? I'd learned very, very early in life not to give anyone a rental unit in my head space, because they could end up with squatter's rights. Put a padlock on your brain and keep that shit out. And the way I casually brushed off any 4-H taunting, I couldn't help but notice, gave some other kids "permission" to join.

Let me be very clear about how important 4-H was to me: it was my personal equivalent to an MBA. From healthy living to agriculture, communications, and community service to science and technology, 4-H teaches skills we can use in real life. The program continues to grow true leaders and encourages us all to communicate with one another by lifting our heads up from our phones and having actual conversations. When I was a child, it wasn't the iPhone that stood in my way (it had yet to be invented). I had other challenges.

School was one. Don't get me wrong. I liked school. I loved history, health, and science. It goes without saying that I aced phys ed. There wasn't a sport or a fitness activity I wouldn't tackle like I owned it. And since I was motivated by success, I studied when I needed to because I wanted good marks. But my corrected homework looked like a toddler on sugar overload had been set loose with a red crayon. One of my early report cards said "Mandy has difficulty with spelling." Nice. I was further blessed with the inability to write down numbers in their intended order. (*That's* a handy trait for a future business owner.)

As it turns out, I had—correction, I have—dyslexia. (I think that's how you spell it.) Back then, sadly, no one understood it. But my teachers were always kind and never made me feel inferior. When I was in grades four and five, a nice man with a wonderful beard would pop his head into my homeroom class and say, "Mandy, are you ready?" He pulled me out of class to work one-on-one with me every day. And though I can't say much changed with my spelling and numerical ability, he was always patient and kind. I somehow knew he wanted to help.

Imagine my surprise when, more than three-and-a-half decades later, the same nice man contacted me. He'd read a story about me in the *Globe and Mail*. I'd been named Canada's Most Admired CEO, an award presented by the management consulting firm Waterstone Human Capital. He was compelled to reach out. In that kind, gentle voice I remembered from my childhood, he said, "Mandy, I always knew you'd be brilliant and would do something amazing. I didn't know how to tell you that being dyslexic wasn't a handicap, and that we had to teach you differently."

He felt the need, so many years later, to seek me out and explain that. Kindness like that goes a long way.

Everyone struggles with something growing up. Sometimes those struggles can send a kid off the rails. Dyslexia, I know now, has the potential to do that. If not for the kindness of my teachers, and if not for activities like sports and 4-H—where I knew I could excel, where I built my confidence with every challenge I took on, and perhaps most importantly, where I instinctively felt I belonged—those heavily marked-up tests and assignments might have done me far more damage than they did.

So, yes, spelling seemed beyond my grasp. But I had other things on my mind. I had Plum. It was my job to feed her each day, to make sure she was cleaned and groomed, to take her for walks on a lead, and—this was the kicker—to train her.

"In the summer," Jordan had explained when he'd brought me to the field to "choose" my calf, "when the exhibition is on, you'll be showing her in a ring with other 4-H members and their calves."

I nodded, my eyes on the animals but my sights already on the competition ahead. I said, "It's on like Donkey Kong!"

Picture, if you will, an awkward eleven-year-old trying to put a rope halter on a three-month-old calf in a very narrow stall, with all the other "Plums" around, all of them dropping turds like it's D-Day while trying to moo in tune.

Plum and I finally made it into the yard. We got as far as the calf barn. Then someone fired up the tractor. The exhaust choked loudly, and Plum slid out of my sad excuse for a rope halter like a raw egg dripping through my fingers. She took off through the field. I gave chase.

Plum showed no sign of slowing. She had almost made it to the main road in our rural community when, after watching this exhibition with great delight, Matt, the son of the brothers who owned the dairy farm we were on, came to the rescue. He helped me save Plum from becoming roadkill, then showed me how to properly fasten the rope halter. Crisis averted. He quietly advised me to keep her away from loud noises at this point in our training. Thanks.

I went home feeling defeated. We all experience such days. But it was nothing a good night's sleep couldn't fix.

The next morning, I went back to the farm, steeled myself, and followed Matt's directions with the halter. I walked Plum around the yard without incident. Success! I had this calf completely under control. We circled back to the barn. While we were entering the stall, Plum kicked me in the thigh. She was only young, but then, so was I. It was like being kicked in the teeth by a Clydesdale. I danced around, waiting for the pain to take a hike, when one of the other brothers, Darryl, walked toward me, a big smile on his face.

"Renne! You have to show her who's boss or she'll send you home with a lot more bruises. And you're gonna need a pair of steel-toed boots or she'll break your toes, too. Wait here," he commanded.

A few minutes later he came back with a shitty-looking pair of boots plus a large pair of socks. "These belonged to my son. Put them on, and you'll be fine around here."

Then he walked away.

One of the best things about the 4-H leaders was that they didn't coddle us. They taught independence, which often as not amounts to what I call the "suck it up" approach to life.

Three bruises, three rodeo scenes, and three months later, Plum and I were ready for competition. The day had arrived when, I figured, with all the work I had done, I could win this. I headed to the arena full of confidence.

But Plum was not in the mood to be shown off. It turns out I hadn't shown her who was boss after all, a fact that was obvious to the judge. I lost the competition. I didn't even place. Teddy, one of my best friends and another 4-H kid, lived down the street from Plum's farm and entered every competition. I knew she'd be a formidable opponent, and I was right. Teddy and her calf took the top prize.

We rejoiced in her win together, but I wasn't going away quietly. The childhood trait that served me best was perseverance.

A year later, I was back with a new Plum—this one was called Annie, after my new idol, Annie Lennox. Annie and I, I'm still proud to say, cleaned up the ribbon ring that year. I left that massive dirt arena with a smile that would rival Pacman's.

Working with animals wasn't the only skill I learned at 4-H. Public speaking may be among the top three fears of most people, but 4-H erased that fear in me with encouragement, practice, and cool tips on how to stand in front of people without shaking like a bowl of unset Jello.

The ability to communicate with others, to not feel like you can't get air into your lungs when you have to address a crowd, to stand confidently and share with others, including peers—the scariest group of all—that is a massive feat. That's what programs like 4-H offer, giving those who have mastered the skills an edge, an advantage in life.

I can't overstate the importance the 4-H program played in my life. It was a safe place for me to learn that I could be me, nothing more, nothing less—just a better me. I've always said that if we made 4-H compulsory for all kids, we'd change the face of the future.

In the spring of my final year in high school, our class's upcoming graduation was the talk of the town. But I couldn't have cared less about that cap-and-gown event. In my mind, I'd already moved on. There was never any question about me continuing on in school. University, as the next logical step for most of my classmates, was not an option. Our family's financial situation didn't easily allow for that opportunity. Even if I were to go, powered by student loans, I'd find myself in the broke-ass category of everyone else who chose that path. I had no intention of adding long-term debt to my life plan.

Besides, though I had the marks and the acumen, academia held zero appeal for me. Instead, all I could think about was how I was going to make enough money to get me started in the trades.

Plan A: make the most of my farming skills. By then, my reputation among the local farmers as a reliable, hard worker was established. Word-of-mouth references resulted in job offers from two well-established farms. Their owners were keen to put me to work as soon as possible.

There was no coin toss—I accepted both offers. Never say no to a good opportunity.

When it came time to leave, I packed everything I could fit into that old hockey bag. My mind raced. I looked around my room, the only space in the house that was all mine. I had my bed, my clothing, and my stereo—and a lock on the door that I knew worked. I was leaving all this behind for a place and people I didn't know. Where would I sleep? What would it be like to live in the midst of an entirely different family? I was reasonably sure I was giving up the luxury of the heated waterbed I'd had for three years.

That bed was a gift from my boyfriend. I was crazy about him, or as crazy as a person not attracted to the opposite sex (but not yet quite understanding what the heck that was about) could be. His family had made it big in the fishing industry, and I'll never forget the look on Pup's face when that boyfriend showed up with this extravagant gift bought with money Pup could only dream of. It was a tense moment. I managed to smooth it over, probably because of all the practice I'd had growing up in a household often rocked by flaring tempers.

I slung that heavy bag over my shoulder, took one last look around my room, and off I went.

The dairy farm was my first stop—that was where I'd be living. The owner, Debbie, was not a woman to be crossed: fierce, intelligent, and self-made. She demanded respect if you wanted to be part of her immediate force field, but she also appreciated determination and a work ethic. She took an immediate liking to me. She appreciated, she said, my ambition. When she asked about my future plans, I was blunt: I wouldn't be going to university, and I needed to make money. It was that simple.

She offered me room and board—no money. Instead, she said she would teach me everything she knew. That would put zero dent in my immediate financial needs, but my brain did a quick calculation and the offer, I knew, had merit, albeit with the faint scent of manure. While I felt a bit skeptical, I thought since she, too, had come from a humble background, surely she would not take advantage of me. I agreed to her terms.

The owner of the other farm was quite a bit younger—and, lo and behold, my attraction to her was intense. "Gay" stopped rolling around vaguely in my mind and took centre stage.

I turned on the Mandy charm.

I have never been one to play games, and, thankfully, she appreciated my straightforward, honest approach and responded in the best possible manner. This exploration of sexuality was new territory for me, and, while I was nervous, I could feel the shift—I was becoming even *more* me. There's a freedom that arrives with finally coming to terms with who you really are and having the guts to live it out.

She was a little older than me, and it was obvious she knew her way around the world of flirting—and more. One day, she invited me to join her for dinner after my farm chores were done. It turned out "dinner" for her meant something other than meat and potatoes. Or maybe I'd gotten the invitation wrong and she had meant "dessert."

She came down the stairs in a gorgeous silky shirt, sat seductively in front of me, and asked me to rub her shoulders. I was paralyzed—what the hell do I do? That feeling quickly passed, and one thing led to another. I woke up the next morning, ankles quivering and my toes still curled. I knew I wanted more of this woman.

What we had from day one was a love affair, in every sense of the word. Until it wasn't. About a year into what we thought was our secret relationship, her mother caught us "together" and told her daughter that what we were doing was nothing but a phase we were going through. I felt like I'd been jabbed in the ribcage with a steak knife. I was sad, hurt, afraid that she'd walk away from what we had. I'd never experienced anyone questioning my intentions, and it hurt to the core.

It's funny how those bumps in the road, detours, setbacks in our lives are the very things that take us closer to where we are meant to be.

By the end of my tenure at both farms, I was a veteran cowhand, stable hand, and general farming apprentice. I'd dealt with pregnancies, rudder infections, haying, and feed salesmen. I was no stranger to sixteen-hour workdays, with naps stolen in the dead of the afternoon, between milkings. I had my first real business conversations with Debbie. She'd say, "So what are you going to do when you figure out what you're going to do?" And we'd get into it. She'd tell me things like, "You have a real gift for people." And, on the question of whether, like everyone else I knew, I should go to university, "You sure as hell aren't going to do that."

We meet many different people on our journeys, and the key is to learn from every single one. I'd worked hard on that farm, but I was aware on some level that my contributions were worth more than the room and board I'd agreed to in our deal. Debbie was using me. She thought, because I was young and inexperienced, she could do that.

If I was ever going to move on, I needed real cash in hand. I needed cash, period, for basic stuff, like clothes. I took a side job at a farm in Milford for a young guy and his uncle—but the old guy harassed me. He felt me up. He would not leave me alone.

Good thing I was smart enough to have arranged to take unpaid days off when I could get paying work in Halifax. Through friends, I got a gig working with a crew laying a hardwood floor in a Halifax restaurant. That job led me to some cleaning jobs in the pub and restaurant industry. That meant night shifts, but what did I care? Sign me up! I was making more money in commercial cleaning than I ever could have working on the farms.

That was when I began to understand the limitless potential in the trades—and also that, in that world, if you showed up, if you worked quickly and well, you were gold. You were prized. Because too many people in that industry didn't. This was my ticket away from the farms: the drama of the love affair on one farm, the lack of pay on the other, the disgusting harassment by the uncle on the third, and, finally, the sense of being treated with no respect, like "just" a farmhand. How could these farmers treat me respectfully when they didn't see their own value? Without them, we don't eat. But they'd absorbed the stupid-ass attitude that they're "only" farmers. I saw that perception, the poison in it, and the fundamental flaw. It hit me in the face every day.

I promised myself I would never treat my people the way I'd been treated working on farms. Because I knew by then that, no doubt in my mind, I *would* have workers. That I would build a business, and I'd do it right.

———

The farmer I'd fallen for and I respectfully disagreed with her mother. We were more than a phase. We continued our affair for a time, one that was tumultuous for me. I was also dealing with the mental anguish of finally understanding I was gay. It wasn't mainstream to be gay. I'd always known I was different, but I was now officially way more "different" than I'd ever guessed. It was a monumental truth to digest.

But the more work I took on in Halifax and the more connections I made there, the more another world opened up.

It didn't take me long to learn that, on Canada's East Coast, Halifax was the epicentre of gayness. The city was home to a massive gay community. There were gay bars and gay ball teams. It was like being a worshipper of hockey your whole life and then, all of a sudden, someone takes you to the Hockey Hall of Fame and your favourite players are there, sitting around a table, inviting you to join them.

I won't make excuses for what happened next. How in the hell was I supposed to know Halifax was a freaking cesspool of women? And that I was a hound dog? The farmer and I wound up going our separate ways, but both better people for having spent that year together.

Once again, I was heading into new territory. I'd learned a lot on the farms, and even more from my farmer romance. Any inhibitions I had about women were gone. I was bolder, confident in my sexuality, and in the so-called "male" part of me that boldly went after what it wanted. I was loving my new "country girl in the big city with no rules" reality.

Meanwhile, I was building a network of friends and acquaintances who, it turned out, could either lead me to jobs or help me fulfill them. I was playing sports. And, because Halifax was such a university town, I'd say to my friends on a team, I've got these gigs cleaning the pubs downtown (at Halifax institutions like the Granite Brewery, the Argyle, the Split Crow)—I need help. Any takers? And they'd look at their class schedules and say, "Yeah, I'll work from Monday to Thursday." That's how I rounded up my staff. At the same time, someone would say, "My sister's looking for some work done on her house" or "My brother's a carpenter."

I recognized quickly that my lens on the world of the trades, and the opportunities it offered, was rare. I witnessed entitlement every day: people saying "Yeah, okay, I'll do this." Maybe showing up, maybe not. Not taking it seriously—either the work opportunity *or* the commitment they'd made. They weren't quick to get back to people. So I'd just show up onsite and get to work. I'd ask when they needed a quote and give it to them by that time. And people were enamoured with me. They'd say, "You're friendly" and "You're fun" and "You perform." It was as if nobody'd ever met someone who was ambitious and who also had a personality.

That was how I built my business. I'd say to people, "If you're not completely happy with what I'm doing here, I'll do it for free." And then I made sure they were happy. It wasn't long before all I heard was *ka-ching, ka-ching.*

4

MAKE GOOD ON YOUR OUTRAGEOUS PROMISE

The wood floors were magnificent. I wanted to lay my face down across those beauties. I wanted to give them a gentle massage.

The flooring's monetary value was obvious, but so was its sentimental value. A meticulously executed plan was in order. As was a team. I needed hands. It was time to call home. My brother rounded up five guys who were willing to come to Halifax for a couple of weeks. These were the guys who, during the summer, would take on only enough odd jobs to get by. This one was an easy sell: it was an excuse to hit the city for a while. My only rule for them at night was: I don't care how much beer you drink, just make sure you show up at 7 o'clock and you're in good condition to work.

Next, I would need some space to practise before I touched one inch of those precious floors. I visited a friend who had a business in the local industrial park and offered him a fee to use the back of his warehouse.

I purchased hardwood that closely matched the original wood in the client's home and rented appropriate equipment: a drum sander, an orbital sander, an edging machine. With the test flooring laid out on the warehouse floor, the process began. I'd have to test wood finishes, master the equipment, understand dry times, and make damn sure this would work. We sanded, prepped, and applied the finishing products. "Close but no cigar" was not an option. Perfection was the goal.

My friend who'd rented me the warehouse space was damn curious. He hung around watching us for a while. Finally, he asked, "What the heck are you doing, Rennehan?"

"Listen," I told him, "I can't make a mistake here. I spent a quarter of what I should make on this job on the testing materials in order to get this job done right."

We both laughed. It was an expensive "test." But I stood to lose a whole lot more, including the reputation I was starting to build, if I failed.

Through the illustrious grapevine, I'd heard there was a job in Halifax with a very wealthy, prestigious family, and that the job involved some Brazilian cherry floors, an exotic hardwood that was rare in the Maritime home-building industry, an over-the-top luxury. The clients wanted their floors sanded and refinished.

I answered the ad. Every bone in my body said I had to be onsite for this project. The company took me on. I took time off from my job at the Milford farm—where I hated being anyway—and showed up on the job site early, ready to go.

A team of six was on the roster. Only four of us showed up, two of them hung over. The one sober guy was so lazy, he was useless. That left just me. Unbelievable, and yet not surprising. I'd already seen far too much of this bullshit in my limited on-the-job experience.

Most clients tell the crew what they want done, then walk away. Not this guy. The homeowner had taken a keen interest in the project, likely because of the value of the rare wood and the expertise I'm sure he knew it would take to protect his investment. Less than forty-eight hours in, he approached me. He didn't look happy, and he didn't mince words.

"You're the only one who has shown up on time and with a great attitude," he said. "And you're the only one that seems to be getting anything done."

He paused. I said nothing.

Then he asked, "Can you do this job?"

I thought, *I'm eighteen, I haven't got a freaking clue what I'm doing, but I know I can pull this off.*

I replied, calmly and confidently, "I can absolutely do this job. But I'm gonna need twelve days, your keys, and your credit card, sir."

My new client called his wife. He told her he couldn't believe he was handing the credit card over, no questions asked, to this girl from Yarmouth. "Her name's Mandy," he said, laughing. "I don't even know how to describe her to you!"

The family was leaving for the Bahamas the next day, and the job was set to be finished by their return, less than two weeks later. The details ironed out, the man with the exotic wood flooring handed me his credit card and house key. I tucked them safely into my front shirt pocket, and we shook hands to seal the deal.

Now all I had to do was figure out how to execute the job.

I had been in my customary "watch" mode, paying close attention to everything the contractors were doing, hoping to gain enough knowledge to one day take on a job like this myself. That time had come much sooner than anticipated. I was far from being an expert floor finisher, but I was determined to complete the job as adeptly as any seasoned specialist in the field.

In our rented warehouse with our rented equipment, we experimented on white oak, red oak, birch, maple, and knotty pine. We tried out different sanding grits on different woods. There were no how-to YouTube videos back then. You had to learn by trial and error. I knew enough to understand that the wood we'd be working with, that costly Brazilian cherry, was very unforgiving. It's temperamental in cold climates. It's softer than an ordinary hardwood, so it would show any flaws. We wouldn't be going near that precious wood until I was damn sure we knew our shit.

The last step in our test process was to seal the sample wood we were working with. I'd heard about a guy in Wisconsin who was said to have the best wood sealant products on the market.

"I need your polyurethane," I told his voicemail.

He didn't return my first, second, or third calls. To be fair, he didn't know the Bear drill: that I would keep hitting redial. Canada, much less Nova Scotia, meant nothing to our American friends back then. How to convince this Wisconsin guy to accept the fact that a persistent woman from Nova Scotia wanted his product, and that she should be taken seriously?

Finally, I left him a respectful Rennehan rant: "Listen, I am one built, athletic woman here in Nova Scotia, and if you don't answer the damn phone, I'm gonna fly to Wisconsin and have this conversation with you in person."

He returned my call.

Fred, my bald, bright-eyed angel from Wisconsin, didn't just fly the product up to Halifax—he came with it. It's not as if his urethane needed an escort. It's top-quality stuff, but it's not like a rare artwork that you'd have to keep under constant guard. Fred made the trip, I'm convinced, out of sheer curiosity.

In the warehouse, he watched me intently for a couple of hours as I applied his superior product to the wood. Then he took the T-bar and showed me some great tricks in application, which is a craft of its own. I was so grateful. It took a couple of attempts, but eventually I smiled at the results. It was perfect!

Fred shared my excitement, and we had a good chuckle. We knew this was the beginning of a great marriage without the sex, something that was becoming a thing in my trades world, given I was one of very few gay females in the industry. To this day, Fred and I are great friends, and we always laugh as he tells the story about the little shit from Nova Scotia who kept burning through his phone line, filling his voicemail, with no sign of giving up.

Practice run complete, it was time to relocate from the warehouse to that beautiful home and its gorgeous dark-cherry floors. We were ready to go. We worked in portions of the floor. Sand a section off, get it prepped, lay the sealer down. It was very light. When we started to work on the next part, we were like, *Holy shit! This isn't the same colour. It's not red anymore. It's orange!*

I freaked out. I thought somehow we'd stained the floor. I sent one of the guys who was working with us out to the local industrial park: "Get your ass over to Kent Building Supplies and see if you can find anybody who knows anything about floors or Brazilian cherry."

I started calling around to sanding companies. Knowing what I know now, I'd have found a sanding company from the outset to do the work with me, rather than hiring a bunch of boys from Yarmouth—as new to flooring as I was. But that's the point. I didn't know what I know now. I knew nothing. Except how to learn on the fly. And how to ask questions.

Important skills, my friend.

I found a sanding company in Mahone Bay—that's down the South Shore of Nova Scotia—a husband-and-wife team. I played I was a homeowner interested in installing new floors and looking for advice about this rare wood. The man said he'd once done a Brazilian cherry floor. Only one. "And, you know, it's not the same colour when you're through, but my God it's the same kind of beautiful."

I thought, *Oh, thank God.* And he was right. The thing about Brazilian cherry is that its outer layer takes on a red tint from the sun. When you sand that off, you get a very light, very beautiful orange patina. Over time, it darkens to its original red.

My team completed the floors in ten days. I had barely eaten or slept, and all I wanted to do was drop to the floor and cry. But first, I needed to know that I had accomplished what I had set out to do—most importantly, that I'd met my client's expectations. The owner had returned from holiday, and he arrived to look over our work. As he stared at the floor, I gulped and asked, "Are you happy with what you see?"

He turned to me, and I could swear there was a tear in his eye. "Mandy, I never dreamed in a million years you'd get it done, let alone this early. And I certainly never dreamed that it would look like this."

The learning curve on this job had been steep, the sweat equity enormous. But it was worth it. I had passed with flying colours. I was elated. I blurted out, "That's good, because I never made a cent."

It was the truth. The supplies and tradespeople had cost me that much. What happened next was unexpected. He firmly let me know, "Oh, Mandy, you're going to get what I said—and more."

I hadn't been frank so that he'd pay me more than the agreed-on amount. A deal is a deal, and holding to an agreement speaks to one's integrity. But because I had committed from the very beginning of my career to being transparent with everyone I dealt with, it was important to me that he have all the facts, and that included costs.

My honesty paid off. It didn't hurt, of course, that it was tied to a job well done. He paid me double—and accelerated the heck out of my business trajectory.

From that first sanding job, I knew I was going to be the leader: that I would build a company in charge of all the subtrades. I would take on the jobs—be they floors, full renovations, what-have-you—and plan, and staff, and execute. Even though I wanted to drop dead of exhaustion, I had never been so excited in my life. To lead a job and to lead people. This was my gift.

Nothing teaches faster than onsite experience, so I began calling local contractors and trying to convince them to let me work with them for free, to get the experience I needed. Not to *be* a carpenter or plumber or electrician—but to understand, when I was the one in charge, what those jobs involved. So I could recognize, at a glance, the difference between a skilled and careful rooflayer and one who was cutting corners. So I would know what kind of supplies and support every skilled tradesperson on my team would need to be able to do their jobs quickly, comfortably, safely, and well.

That's right: I offered to work at no charge. Telling someone you'll work for free is cause enough for them to think it's a prank and hang up, but a young female making that call? No way was I taken seriously at first. But I kept calling until they gave in.

"Listen," I'd say, determined to get onto those worksites. "You're going to like me. I'm a quick learner, and I will add value to whatever you're working on. I'll haul everything out of the trucks, do all the shit work, just so I can understand the fundamentals of what you're doing. I guarantee I'll understand it enough to be a real help to you and not a nuisance."

One time I told the guy on the other end of the phone, "If I'm not better than your best worker after two nights, then I'll pay *you*." I didn't have any damn money, but it was worth a try. After that beautiful pitch, the phone line still went silent.

Ninety-nine percent of the time I was talking to guys, and I think some of them eventually gave in just so they could prove girls didn't belong in construction. The joke was on them. Usually, they would end up offering me employment. Quite a nice change in attitude, boys. It was a start.

I bounced around in this way, from trade to trade to trade, gaining an understanding of the fundamentals. Every two or three months I'd choose a different area of trades: HVAC, roofing, plumbing, concrete, and so on. I covered as many as I could. I pulled wire in commercial buildings, through different studding, three or four hundred feet. I worked alongside electricians and learned why they used this many volts; why we'd run this much wire from this 15-amp circuit. On masonry sites I learned how crucial it is that everything's level and plumb: this is a wall that's going to hold a roof up. I learned how physically demanding roofing is; the real, everyday risk involved in that kind of work; and the importance of care and precision, especially when installing vents and skylights. You need to calculate meticulously or people's homes are going to leak. I learned that plumbing is shit rolling downhill for real—how most people don't realize a house needs to be engineered for the plumbing to function properly. Then there's carpentry. Talk about artists!

What I learned on every site, no matter the skill or trade, was the complexity and knowledge involved in the work. How intelligent, patient, and skilled you need to be to do the work well. Why it takes, for example, three or four years to become a certified electrician. The more I learned, the more addicted I became to wanting to know more.

Just as crucial as the practical skills I was picking up, was the way I saw my persistence pay off. When you know you have something to offer, don't let a "hang up" stop you. Make them listen. Hit redial. Then hit it again. And again. Sooner or later, you'll wear them down.

Thankfully, I have a photographic memory: I see it, remember it, then do it. A lot of listening and hard work would warm the boys up to me. Then, I'd nonchalantly offer to do a task and have them watch, instead of the other way around. Letting them think it was their idea helped.

"I'll run the wire tonight and you inspect it," I'd say, as if it was already a done deal. Don't let them see you sweat, and don't give them an option. I may not have known what I was doing right off the bat, but dammit, I always found a way to get the jobs done, and done well. I came through every time. Eventually, the tables turned, and contractors started calling me to help on their job sites. "Rennehan, you wanna come out tonight?"

Nothing could keep me away. I was a sponge. I watched, I listened, I learned, taking it all in. That's how I began to master the skills, and it's also how I began to build my network.

At first, I was watching every single move to learn the practical tools of the trade. But it wasn't long before the tactical side of my brain went into overdrive. I began to see how these companies could be making so much more money if they did things differently. Wasted time and materials made my skin crawl. Little shortcuts pissed me off so badly I didn't know what to do with myself. And I came to believe that companies entirely controlled and managed by men, with no women in the mix, lacked the female skills or mindset to understand the potential of good organization—tactics like breaking a job into phases, and more, that would bring a business to the next level.

Oh, sure, the jobs always got done. But I couldn't wait to throw the ugly-ass, progress-halting status quo out the fucking window. My way of thinking was different. If I were in charge—*when* I was finally in charge—I'd get things done more efficiently, with cost savings and a far prettier bottom line.

5

BUILD A BUSINESS THAT WILL MAKE YOU, NOT BREAK YOU

That beautiful, used, grey 1988 Mazda B2000 was the bomb.

She was all mine, and not a moment too soon.

With the successful completion of the job on the fancy wood floors, my name had begun to spread, like a bad fart, throughout the city and beyond. What I'd given the client and his family surpassed their expectations, and they willingly shared the story about this feisty girl from Yarmouth in maintenance and construction, who followed through on her promises—and then some. Their endorsement carried a great deal of weight.

One of the best rewards that came out of the word-of-mouth endorsements was that working without pay could finally come to an end. Even the retail giants started to come knocking. It was risky, and some would even call it foolish, but I have never regretted one second of the time I spent working for free. It provided me with an education that I would not otherwise have been able to afford, and it translated into a reputation that continues to serve me well.

As more paying work came along, I began to build up my own bank of equipment. Every level of success you achieve comes with new requirements. Suddenly, I desperately needed a truck to get me and all my gear to job sites. How difficult could purchasing a truck be? Surely bankers would see my exceptional talent and be excited to lend me the money. So off to the bank I went for my first vehicle loan.

Actually, I went to every bank in Halifax. Nobody—*nobody*— would lend me the money. It turns out "potential," "talent," and "self-confidence" don't count as collateral.

I spoke with every bank employee who'd listen until I finally found someone who would at least consider providing the loan. I could tell this female banker really wanted to lend me the money, but she couldn't bend the rules to make it happen.

I looked her square in the face and said, "If you will just give me a chance, I'll pay this truck off in six months, not three years. I promise I'll come in here every day, and every day I'll give you more money than you want."

I meant it. Her eyes welled up with tears.

"I need this," I told her. "I don't have parents to go to. I don't have anybody who can help me. I need you to find a way to lend me the money. And you need to trust me."

Once in a while there's someone who believes in you as much as you believe in yourself. I don't know how, but she found a way to lend me the money.

True to my word, I paid the truck off in five months. The lender took me out for what I thought was a congratulatory lunch—until she told me off.

Huh?

Over lunch, she served me a terse lesson on how banks make their money. It had never occurred to me that the bank wouldn't want its money back as quickly as possible, especially since that's exactly what I'd promised. I'd meant that promise, and I kept it. So whether they liked it or not, that truck was fully paid for in record time.

One more purchase would make the truck complete: I needed a car phone. For months, I put aside every single penny I earned for that all-important purchase. I didn't "need" a new pair of jeans or a new pair of boots. Heck, I didn't even need a good meal as much as I needed that phone. It cost me $299 and was so big it looked like a couple of encyclopedia volumes. You couldn't have three people in the front of my truck: just me, one passenger, and the phone. I also armed myself with two pagers, one business and one personal. Geared up with all these devices, I looked like Rambo with hand grenades.

But there was a problem. While the pagers would buzz anywhere, that darn monstrosity of a phone would work only in a vehicle, plugged into the cigarette lighter.

Being the age I was, and the ambitious, crazy little shit I was, there was no damn way I was going to miss one single call from current or potential clients. So, while I paid rent on my apartment faithfully each month, I spent most nights in my truck. It was uncomfortable, and I had cramps in body parts I didn't even know existed. My staff used to beat on the window in the morning.

But I had to be absolutely certain I could be tracked down immediately by anyone who needed me because people were starting to talk about me and my work.

Then, miracle of miracles, the Motorola gods came out with the almighty flip phone. It was astonishing. Overnight, my business doubled. I was gradually adding commercial flooring and other jobs—some for major chains—to my roster of cleaning contracts. And I didn't have to stay glued to my truck.

Of course, too much of a good thing is not so great.

Through the reputation I was building with my pub-cleaning contracts, I got a call from Canada Post and took on their janitorial contract for the local area. Huge, right? It gets better. Onsite, I kept hearing the guys there say things like, "Our lighting keeps going out." *I can fix that*, I thought.

So I asked them, "Can I get on your bid list for lighting?"

It turned out there was an RFP open—a "request for proposals." One of them gave a me a confused look. "But you're doing janitorial."

"I can do it all," I told him. Then I flashed him my I-dare-you-to-underestimate-me smile.

But I was nineteen, and I'd never filled out an RFP. You have to lay everything out, in detail: your plan, how much money you're making, what your projections are. I'd never done a projection in my life. Inexperience aside, my dyslexia wasn't exactly a super-power in the circumstances. I went to my bookkeeper and asked for help. (Yes, at nineteen I already needed a bookkeeper.) She said, "I'm not a contractor." I countered with, "You don't need to be." She understood numbers, and she understood me. I knew she had the patience to take me through it, to fill in the financial forms thoroughly and carefully. I paid her hourly to sit with me. That RFP was one of the most painful processes I went through as a budding entrepreneur. Still, to this day, I hate them. My mind doesn't compute that way.

This is how my mind works: I took a week and drove to the twenty-two locations the RFP covered. I wanted to see how many fluorescents they had, ballasts, everything involved in keeping the electrical in shape. I was able to do a quick scout at each building and remember what I saw (that photographic memory). Then I went to three local electricians and asked them what their pricing would be if I could get them this volume of work. You'd need to hire another electrician and apprentice to work with me, I told them, but I'll manage everything. They were small shops, mostly taking residential calls or bidding various contracts; they'd never have dreamed of being part of an RFP like this. I think they thought I was full of shit. Like, *How is this girl going to get this contract?*

This is how: on my RFP, instead of including a fee for each service call, I proposed a scheduled preventive maintenance call once a month. They'd be paying a little more upfront, but they'd save 20 percent at the end of the year. I was organized. I was thinking cleverly inside an industry that had never seen that kind of thinking. I gave them a plan for something that never had a plan before.

And it got me in the door.

But getting in the door meant fulfilling my promises—actually ramping *up* the intensity. When you win the RFP, that's when things start to move.

So much was at stake, on that RFP and with all my other contracts, I figured I didn't have time to focus on my well-being. All I cared about was not missing a call, and doing as much work as I could possibly take on. Today we know better, so we do better. But in the early days of building my business, I lived my life between my truck, my phone, and the job sites. The pace just about killed me.

Over one two-week period, I felt even more tired than usual. I also had a nasty-looking rash on my abdomen that hurt like hell. It took a well-meaning friend to tell me it might be serious and that I should see a doctor.

"You look like hell, you're asleep while driving, and you refuse to admit anything's wrong. And that rash," he said. "Shit, Mandy."

We were finishing up a contract with Office Depot that night, and at about 2 a.m., my flooring guy stopped me. "Okay, Mandy, you look horrible, and there's blood on the front of your shirt!"

"Yes, and the district manager is coming for a walk-through in the morning," I told him.

He wasn't having it. "Get your ass to outpatients. Jimmy and I will finish this job."

I heard what he was saying, but it didn't compute. I was in charge here. *I* was the one who made sure we finished the job.

He must have seen the disbelief on my face. "I promise you, Mandy, when the DM walks in, we will all look like superstars."

Finally, reluctantly, I gave in. I was more worried about my customer than I was about the blood stain on my shirt, but off to the hospital I went. Six hours and five tests later, my very efficient emergency doctor told me I had mono and a nasty case of shingles.

Shingles, he said, was rare for someone my age. "Did you have chicken pox as a kid?"

Damned if I could remember that. "I think so," I responded.

"Chronic stress is the only thing that would bring a case of shingles on this bad, and mono is its cousin." He looked awfully concerned, and maybe just a bit bewildered. "How are you even functioning?"

I gave the good doctor a thin version of my chubby story about building the business, finding new clients, and so on. He firmly told me I'd need to take it easy for the next month to six weeks.

I felt like all the air had been sucked from the room. "I can't do that. It's impossible. I'll lose my clients."

He didn't say, bless him, that if I never got healthy I'd lose all my clients anyway. But deep down, despite my desperation, I knew it. So I made a conscious, albeit difficult, effort to slow down. I hired someone for the next six weeks so I wouldn't have to do any heavy lifting on the job.

The anxiety was excruciating. My mind raced to figure out how long I could pay the extra guy, when I would feel better, if I would lose any clients. When you're in business, especially in the early going, sickness does not seem like an option. But I *was* sick. So, option or not, I had to face reality.

One night, after the first round of pills, I lay in bed and actually fell asleep. I woke up an hour past my usual time, and I do believe that's when I experienced my first panic attack.

I called Dean, the guy I had put in charge of our most recent job, to see if the crew was downtown starting the work on the pubs. I called him eight times. I was getting into my Jeep when my cell phone finally rang.

"Are you trying to get me?" Dean asked, a bit of frustration in his voice.

"Yes, and you weren't answering!"

"Mandy, didn't you see the weather? It's blowing hard out there, and the team is moving equipment from the truck. And you're sup-posed to be sleeping. So stop calling me, go back to bed, and I'll fill you in later."

It looked like I had no choice but to do as he said.

"You're a good man, Charlie Brown," I told him.

It would be difficult for me, but I would have to trust that he would do the job in the manner I would. I surrendered to fatigue and my body's need for rest. I closed my eyes and slept, soundly.

———

When I started in business for myself, I was hands-on with every single job, including design, carpentry, plumbing, electrical—and anything else my clients asked for. No matter how big or small the task, this Bear's hands were on it. Heck, I even hand-delivered the paycheques to my staff. It was a standing joke with them. They'd see me coming on a Friday and say, "It must be pay day. Here comes Renne with her chequebook."

They were right. I carried my chequebook under my work clothes because, from day one, everyone who did any work for me was paid before I was—and there's not a soul who can say they weren't paid right away, or within the agreed-on terms. Personal experience had taught me the importance of getting a paycheque on time, and there was no way I'd leave any of my crew hanging.

But clearly, as the company grew, if I was to survive—and be there to run the damn thing—I'd have to change how I did things. This was a different kind of growth than needing to buy a truck and finding the money for it. This was learning how to manage success in order not to lose it. I began to delegate and to manage my funds and my contracts differently. I admit, letting go was harder than I ever thought possible: it meant putting part of my company's reputation in someone else's hands. Shit, to be honest, it was like sending me into a free fall. But I knew it was the right thing to do.

The transition was made much easier by the fact that I had hired every member of my staff personally, so I trusted them to do a job befitting my standards. And because I have been so hands-on in the past—at one time or another I've done every aspect of the job myself—my employees fully trust me to be there for them if any issue, big or small, arises.

Choosing the right people has been a priority—and also a challenge. The problem is, not everyone shares my urgent drive for success. "I need more Mandys!" is a mantra that used to play over in my mind like a broken record. Where the heck were these people hiding? Looking back, I realize I should have strategically sought out people who had five of my top ten qualifications, instead of the full ten. I spent far too much time trying to fit people into the "Mandy" mould. It took me the better part of a decade to accept that each person brings their own skills and value to the table and that, when people are teachable, other skills will emerge.

This mantra has allowed me to stop working so hard that I wind up in bed with mono—*and* shingles. I've built the team I need, so I can focus on running the business from a high level. As a visionary, I am absolutely loving this approach. I make hundreds of decisions every day that affect everyone around me, staff and clients included, but ultimately, I don't have to get into the weeds of each contract we take on. And of course, in the spirit of fun, I don't mind enjoying a cold beer with the team at the successful completion of a job well done.

6

DON'T LET YOUTH (OR ANYONE ELSE'S OPINION) GET BETWEEN YOU AND A PROMISING FIXER-UPPER

B ear," one of my friends said, "you're a bit young now, but you're an awful go-getter."

A group of us were chatting over a beer at The Cellar, the local spot where we'd hang out after work. I was twenty, and since most of my peers had gone to university—and into debt—the new friends I'd made on job sites around Halifax were all older than me. No surprise: they couldn't help giving me advice. Not that I'm complaining. Now and then, that advice nudged me in a direction that would change the course of my life. This was to be one of those times.

"You work your ass off," he continued, "and one day you'll probably have enough money to flip homes."

Aside from the fact that the comment sounded just a bit condescending—most people didn't understand that my age was not a barrier for me—I was curious. "What do you mean by 'flip homes'?"

These guys knew a rapt, willing apprentice when they had one. The whole table got involved. It was relatively simple, they told me. I could buy a house, fix it up, then live in it for a year. That way, I wouldn't have to pay capital gains tax when I sold it for a profit. This sounded all right to me—more than all right. Maybe too good to be true.

I wasn't about to just take their word for it. I like to do my own research. Our friend Google had yet to be invented, so off I went to the accounting section of the local library. I pulled out any books I could find on real estate and finance. They all had a chapter on this capital gains thing my friends had mentioned. It was true: in Canada, if you own a house for at least a year, and you sell it for a profit, you do not have to pay capital gains tax on any of that profit. I was so blown away by the possibilities that I did a happy dance in the library. (Tax laws are nasty, complex, shape-shifting so-and-sos. *Don't try this at home* before checking with your own accountant.) But I couldn't bring myself to trust it—not yet, not fully. I headed straight to the accounting firm my company used. I had to make absolutely sure I wasn't missing any piece of this real estate puzzle before I dove in headfirst—because, frankly, I was standing on the edge of the diving board, ready to take the plunge.

"In your opinion," I asked my accountant, "is this the best way for me to make cash money?"

"Well, yes, if you're good at it. Are you good at it?"

Before I could answer, he added, "That's a lot for you to take on, Mandy, at your age."

Shit, what the hell was with these people? By now I was landing and managing contracts for top-drawer clients like Irving and Canada Post. I didn't need to be babysat. What I needed was cash flow. I mean, seriously, now that I knew exactly what it meant, it made perfect sense for me to purchase, fix up, and flip a home. Who doesn't need a place to eat, shit, and shower? I would be paying rent regardless, so I might as well be paying a mortgage. This wasn't Mozart's first symphony, for Christ's sake.

Now that my mind was made up that I was going to buy my first home, I looked into the real estate market and rules around mortgages. It didn't take long for me to figure out that I'd need 5 percent down on something in the $150,000 range, a place that needed some work and would later sell for a profit. The house would also have to be located in one of Halifax's core areas.

All I was missing was the down payment for the mortgage.

The credit union was my go-to for the money at that time. The first time I'd gone in for a loan, it was for equipment. I'd put my plan on the table, doing my best to impress the guy in commercial lending with my numbers (and my personality). I explained that I would need the equipment loan to get to the next step, but that I had a plan—and it was a solid one. I confidently told him I'd have collateral after I was able to bring on more volume.

But it didn't appear that his ears were working. I remember feeling like I was a pain in his ass the entire meeting, like what I said didn't matter. He didn't give a shit about what I was saying or why I was asking for funds. He just wanted to get to his racquetball game on time. I churned with anxiety.

Suddenly, out of nowhere, not looking me in the eye, he said, "I'll give you the money. Now I have to go, and the ladies downstairs will write up the paperwork."

Up he got. And off he went.

I sat there by myself in his office overlooking Halifax's Kempt Road, thinking, *What in the love of Linda just happened here?* For no reason I could point to, this guy—who didn't seem to have any interest in the case I'd made to him—had agreed to lend me the money I needed to shift my business into third gear.

I wasn't complaining. But had he really just said "yes" because he wanted to shut me up? If so, score one for persistence, Mandy-style.

I went back to the credit union, wondering how hard it could be the second time around.

I filled out a wheelbarrow's worth of paperwork. It showed, to my satisfaction, that I had very little debt or expenses, aside from the cost of business operations. My credit rating was great for my age. I was clearly ready for a mortgage. So I was a bit surprised when the lender said, "Mandy, the lending department is having a difficult time approving your application."

What the holy hell?

"You don't have a T-4 slip proving you have constant income," she told me.

That was the self-employment killer dart landing, bull's eye, between my eyes.

I leaned toward her, determined she would hear me out.

"Listen, I have contracts signed with two of the biggest employers in Nova Scotia: Irving and Canada Post. I have $68,000 in receivables alone, which is bigger than anybody's paycheque my age. Now, explain this to me like I am still in training pants, because I don't understand."

She looked almost frightened. "Mandy, I don't make the rules. And on top of the lack of a T-4, you don't have collateral."

"I'm twenty years old and left home with a suitcase and a damn smile. What kind of collateral do you expect me to have?"

I was trying to hold back my anger, I really was, but I think it would be accurate to say that I roared the question at her. I left the meeting with the same feeling I'd had the last time I had been there: what in the love of Linda had just happened?

It turns out I wasn't the only one who went home and gave the situation a lot of thought. The next day, the lender called and asked me to come back in. When I got there, she told me, "Mandy, you've really left an impression on me. The world needs more ambition and tenacity, and people like you leading the way."

"I appreciate that. Now what are you thinking?" I was cool on the outside but nervous as heck on the inside.

She asked me to confirm that I had $68,000 in receivables. I did. She told me she didn't see a line of credit leveraged against the receivables.

"That's right," I replied. But I was thinking, *What the hell is leveraging and what is a line of credit? Is it the same as an overdraft?* Banking jargon wasn't my forte. But she had my full attention. I was like a baby basset hound primed for an ear rub. "What do you have for me?"

"Do you have a bookkeeper or accountant doing your books?"

"Yes," I replied calmly, and told her my bookkeeper's name.

She asked for the number. "So I can check out your last year's tax return, and this year's as well."

She explained that if she could leverage my receivables with a line of credit, that would give me the down payment and closing costs I would need. And if my bookkeeper could write me a paycheque from the company to substantiate my "income," she knew she could sell the deal to her manager.

I left the credit union blowing kisses at her as the joyous bars of Lionel Richie's "Dancing on the Ceiling" blasted through my mind. Three weeks later I was approved for a mortgage up to $160,000. I had just learned how to "leverage" my money. Mic drop on the status ass quo.

———

One of the fastest-growing spots in the city of Halifax was around Quinpool Road. I went to see a house in the heart of that area. It stood near a hotel that overlooked the Halifax Commons, a huge open green space in the centre of the city. The house had a big deck and no grass, but the minute I walked through the front doors, such trivial shortfalls flew from my mind.

The old pine hadn't been touched, and there was none of what I call the 1980s and 1990s mutilation effect, which had turned once-beautiful homes into ugly-ass renditions of their former selves. There were working fireplaces in the living and dining rooms, both solid mahogany. The rooms were separated by beautiful inch-and-a-quarter sliders, and the plank flooring led to a staircase graced with a turn-of-the-century banister. The ceilings were 10 feet throughout, and the woodwork superb—a testament to the craftsmanship of the house's era. The washroom, which housed a huge claw-foot tub, was roomy enough that the walls couldn't close in on me and take a bite out of my arse. The three bedrooms upstairs had lots of space and were enticingly saying "love me again."

She was magnificent. Yes, she was a she: complicated, intricate, sultry, and sexy. She wasn't lacking room for improvement, by any stretch. When I walked into the kitchen, for example, I was met with holy-crap-hot-lime cabinets. Yes, sir. Bright lime green. But I could see through that, to the possibilities. And the fact that this beautiful saltbox home had survived the historic Halifax explosion was, for me, almost as orgasmic as the structure itself.

When I make up my mind, I make it up. No mulling things over. In short order, that house was mine—all mine.

Except for the $129,000 I owed the bank.

Eventually, I would need to fill the house with some form of furniture. I'd been living with a girlfriend and her roommates, but I worked all the time and creature comforts weren't exactly on my radar. I was putting what money I had into work equipment, my phone, and my pager. That, to me, was the essential stuff. I had a cheap pleather chair of a vaguely Scandinavian design, a box full of wood for the fireplaces, one pillow, and a great big Canadian Tire sleeping bag that I slept in for the first two months. Eventually, someone I knew at one of the pubs I cleaned was moving and gave me their old mattress. In the meantime, I was sleeping on excitement—discomfort be damned.

I loved this project. Loved it. Week by week, month by month, when I wasn't working on my business—or sleeping—I renovated the house. *My* house. My first order of business was to add another washroom, which I knew would bring a huge return on my investment. My carpenter, Ron, and I dug out the basement and poured new footings to add height, because there wasn't enough space, otherwise, to house the changes I wanted to make. I put in a full washroom down there and turned the rest of the space into a rec room.

I remember sitting in that big old house with Bernie, one of my employees at the time. He was high on weed, and I was getting lippy as a result of the twelve-pack of beer I'd put a dent in after a long work week.

"Don't you tell me I can't buy a house!" I said, feigning anger at those who'd told me I wasn't ready, I was too young, I had no leverage. Bernie simply smiled and nodded, his eyes glazed over. We swayed to the Black Crowes hit, "Remedy."

"Remedy" for residential was a tune I was falling for.

Always on the lookout for ways to save funds and access more cash flow, I started renting my rooms to students. Halifax is a university town, which made it easy to do. And I figured that, since I was rarely home, having someone live in my space wouldn't be a bother.

Holy Hannah, was I wrong. I'd arrive home after gruelling days and nights, and walk into a pigpen in every room. Pots, pans, and clothing strewn everywhere. Thinking back on the state of the washroom still makes me queasy.

Clearly, not every idea's going to turn out to be your best. Six months in, I was ready to send them flying out the door off the end of my boot. But I guess you could say this rental shit pushed me to make more money faster, just to get these people the hell out of my space.

It wasn't all for naught. With the money I got from renting out the rooms, I was able to make my loan payments easily and take care of some home improvements besides. In the end, I'd purchased my first home for $137,000 at the age of twenty. One year later, I sold it for $181,000.

Not bad for a "too-young" virgin flipper.

I couldn't buy the next one fast enough. I was hooked. And I learned that I had a natural talent for scoping out homes that needed work but would turn a profit.

The second house I took on was a few blocks away from the first. This one had two flats because, well, this is one girl who learns from her mistakes. There was no way in hell I'd ever again live with people in my personal space. The two flats provided me with a place to lay my head, and with enough cash flow to remodel the space *and* invest back into my commercial endeavours, which were growing fast.

7

CHANNEL YOUR RAGE

I arrived at the job site, a home in a quiet Halifax neighbourhood, bright and early as always. This morning, though, I met with a nasty surprise. The paint I had bought was nowhere to be found.

I asked the owners, who'd been in over the weekend, whether they'd seen any paint cans. They hadn't. I told them I'd bought almost four hundred dollars' worth of paint, and it had vanished. They wondered where it could have gone.

"Only one other person has a key," I said.

Still in the early years of building up my business, I'd been taking on commercial cleaning and maintenance projects in downtown Halifax, which always paid within thirty days. Cash flow was key. I also worked on some home renos in my spare time.

This house, one of my first, was for an older couple—both university professors. The couple was giving their house a facelift, and had hired me for a few particular parts of the job. They had a general contractor looking after the rest.

Hal.

The first time we met, Hal said to me, "Well, it's nice to see a woman onsite here. What are you doing, the cleaning?"

"No," I said, holding back the throat punch. "But I'll do that, too. I'm here to refinish the hardwood. I'm also doing their trim work and painting."

"Well, that's unfortunate, little lady," he said. "Because I should be doing all that, and you'll probably slow me down."

Can you guess where this was leading? Working on that site was one of the most painful experiences I'd endured. Hal was so disorganized that I nearly came out of my skin. The tradespeople he hired didn't show up. When they did show up, they didn't know what they were doing. It kept pushing off my job. What was supposed to take three weeks was stretching into three months. I wanted to shake him.

What I really wanted was to ask the owners just to give me the whole damn job. One day, frustrated by more delays topped with yet more of Hal's insults, I spoke my mind. "Respectfully, Hal, I've lost money because you're so goddamn disorganized you don't even know the war is over. People are showing up here, can't get hold of you, and I'm prepared to go to the owners and tell them I should take over the entire project."

Ever see an old guy with steam coming from his ears? Oh, was Hal angry. He told me there was no way I'd be taking over anything, because the client's sister-in-law was his wife.

Oh, now I understand your qualifications, Hal.

"If you want off this job," he said, "I can make that happen right now."

My blood was boiling. As much as I did not want to back down, I checked myself. I was livid, but I always finish what I start. Besides, I knew first-hand that letting loose in a temper never led to anything good.

I was all of twelve. There was a ball tournament in Kelly's Cove, just outside the town limits. I was on a rep minor baseball team, and we'd beat every local team. I pitched. I had a wicked curve ball and a sneaky slider that my older brother, Chris, had taught me. My fastball was *fast* for this league. Chris told my parents how talented he thought I was. He'd never seen a twelve-year-old boy throw a hardball like that, and certainly not a girl.

During the first inning, I was surprised to see my parents sitting in the bleachers. It was rare for them to come to a game. Seeing them there sent my nerves into high gear. I wanted to impress them, make them proud. Sweat trickled down my back.

The first three batters up, I struck out. My parents, together with the other fans in the stands, roared and banged their feet on the bleachers. I heard Pup yell, "Take that home with ya! That's my girl!"

My first time at bat, I hit a double over the centre fielder's head. Next time, a single to the right. Back on the mound and still on a roll, I walked a batter. My pitches had been in the strike zone; I was sure of that. It was obvious that the fans agreed with me. I kicked the dirt on the mound and heard Pup say, "Shake it off, girl!"

The next batter walked, too. My coach came over to chat with the umpire. The inning finally ended with a pop fly to the left.

I was third up to bat this inning. My teammate Terry hit a double, then Alex hit a single. (Yes, I was the only girl on the team.) So when I got to the batter's box, there were runners on second and third, both in scoring position. We were behind by two runs. If by some wild chance I could hit a home run, it would give us the game. I had been hitting their pitcher all day, so it was a possibility.

First ball was a strike. According to the ump, but not to me. I turned to look at him, and then at Pup. I lowered my head and shook it from side to side. WTF had I done to this man? A moment later I didn't care, because the pitcher threw the ball slow and inside, my absolute favourite. I smoked it over the shortstop's head, between left and centre fields. As I rounded second base, the left fielder tried to cut me off with a pass, but the ball sailed over the second baseman and into right field. The third-base coach was swinging his arms for me to round third.

This was my chance. If I made it home, I'd put us in the lead. I ran my guts out. I saw the ball hit the dirt before I got to home plate. The catcher couldn't get it under control. I slid to the side, stretching my hand across the plate. Safe. No tag.

The umpire yelled, "Out!"

I couldn't believe it. My coach started to question the call. The fans were on their feet booing. I'd had enough. I walked over to the ump, kicked dirt at him and asked if he needed thicker glasses. "You must be blind!" I yelled. I was so angry, it was as though I had gone into a trance.

As they removed me from the game and I walked toward my parents, I wondered how much trouble I was in.

But Pup had tears in his eyes. He looked broken. "Watching you out there, Mandy, you got that from me," he said as we walked to the truck. "That rage, you got it from me!"

I've always believed the way people behave comes from somewhere. My dad had a tumultuous upbringing. He was passed around from foster home to foster home. But one thing he knew he wanted was that elusive love he'd never had growing up. He wanted his own family, and he wanted more than anything to provide for that family.

Sadly, the world's measure of success has always been based on tangibles, the chief one being money: whether you have a house, two cars in the garage, and a cottage. My father sought success on both the world's terms and the "I just want to provide for my family" terms. And while he worked his ass off every day, there were never any guarantees. And my old man could fly into a rage over just about anything, from the whisper of a looming economic downturn to something far less serious. He had a desperate need for everyone to be at least half an hour early for any venture; you weren't getting into his vehicle unless your shoes were clean; and, Holy Hannah, God help anyone in the vicinity if he heard a squeak or rattle of any nature in the house, car, or truck. We'd nicknamed him Ida, after his mother, because, like her, he had to have everything perfect—or there was hell to pay.

But I'd be right there making him smile, doing my best to defuse whatever had soured his mood. Years later, when I was well into my life as a tradeswoman, Pup was helping me renovate a cottage I'd bought. We were on our way back from the hardware store when we heard a rattle in the cupholder. Pup's face turned blood red with frustration. I started talking—about whatever came to mind—to keep him from blowing up. That evening, when we were heading to the local pub for supper, he pointed to both cupholders with a grin. He'd taken old carpet and traced templates out of the circles that held drinks in his truck.

I smiled, grateful that he hadn't lost his mind, like I'd seen him do so many times when we were younger. Then I teased the shit out of him for having the da Vinci of cupholders. After supper, we picked up coffees, just to try out the cupholders. I nearly wet myself when we realized the rattle was on the dash, but he was smitten with his craftsmanship, and I kept praising him for his invention. It worked. We enjoyed the moment and evaded the monster I'd spent my life trying to avoid.

Way back when I was twelve, after my outburst at that ball game, Ma told me that one of the hardest things in life, for a parent, is to watch your kids take on your own negative traits.

For me, it had been a day of reckoning. I would have to learn to control the rage, a side of me that didn't show up often.

Ever since that ball game, I knew it was best to walk away, breathe—whatever it took to let my rage simmer down before I opened my mouth. But it took working on a job site with a guy like Hal to realize that circumstances could still frustrate me to the boiling point; to the point where it was tough to remember, amid the thick fog of my fury, what I'd learned.

I hadn't said everything I'd wanted to say to Hal. I'd forced myself to calm down, bite my tongue. I'd held back.

But not quickly enough. I'd still let frustration get the better of me—for just a moment, a moment too long. That is, long enough to infuriate Hal. And now I was knee deep in the emptiness left behind by four hundred dollars' worth of missing paint.

The homeowner called Hal. He told her that there was no paint. There'd never been any paint. "She's lying," he said.

I didn't know what to say. I could see that these people were having the same problems with him that I was, but because they'd hired him through a family member, they were stuck, or felt they were. They could see in my face that I didn't have any more time for Hal. Nor did I have money for more paint. They asked if we could split the difference to replace it. They didn't know how else to handle the situation. Nor did I.

After that, Hal and his crew did everything to discredit me. They even scratched the floors after we finished them. Why? Because I was competent. I represented confidence. In Hal's mind, no *girl* was going to come in and take over *his* job site. He hated that my team was always on time; he hated that we got the job done; he hated that the clients appreciated our work.

Had I checked my temper and held back my blunt assessment of Hal's performance, I might have avoided his childish but still damaging retaliation. I took that lesson in. There's no place for rage on the job. Let it out another way. Or better yet, channel it into something useful.

8

COMMON SENSE + PLAIN OLD WORK = INNOVATION (REALLY!)

only want to make one phone call, Mandy."

Kate, the building coordinator for Salter Street Films, had introduced herself to me as "Kate with a K." Kate with a K came up to my shoulders, and I wanted to hug the shit out of her. I could hardly believe my ears. It was as if she'd read my mind and found the three magic words to define the business strategy that was simmering in there.

One phone call. All-in-one.

Kate had called and invited me to the Salter Street building on Barrington Street in Halifax, home to popular television productions such as the TV film *Life with Billy* and the political satire *This Hour Has 22 Minutes*. The building was a heritage property that the owners had reportedly dumped a ton of money into.

It was one of the coolest buildings I'd ever been in: a historic brick home that was derelict when the film company had bought it in 1990 for the princely sum of—I kid you not—two dollars. The building had been shored up, rewired, its interior decorative cornice mouldings and rosettes reshaped and replaced; in short, both preserved and restored. It had an art deco flare. It was something out of a movie.

I met Kate by the elevators. As we toured the building, I took in the show posters and photos of Canadian actors. I'd be lying if I said I wasn't a little star struck. Remember, I was twenty-two and still barely a toe removed from my rural roots, from the days when a school trip to Halifax meant the rare and treasured chance to eat at McDonald's.

Dazzled as I was with my surroundings, though, I was way more interested in my conversation with Kate with a K. First of all, I needed to know how she'd found me, so I could do more of *that* marketing.

"Canada Post gave you a great referral," she told me. Aha. See how reputation matters?

"And I'm swamped and could use some help around the building."

What kind of help?

"Okay, Mandy," she began, "We want you to look after all the lighting in this building, and the plumbing if we have an issue. We want you to make sure all mechanical units are serviced for heat and air, and please make sure the building is spotless. The Donovan brothers don't like dirty windows."

Aye, aye, Kate with a K, I thought to myself.

"Oh, and the brothers hate it when the elevator squeaks and is slow, and when there isn't enough salt on the ground when it's slippery outside, and—"

I began to wonder how long this list was going to get. That was when she said it. "I only want to make one phone call, Mandy."

Kate couldn't have known it, but what she had just asked for had been going through my head for the past two years as a way to catapult my business: one phone call, one point of contact. Period. I'd been putting the puzzle pieces together: spotting the voids and filling them; working efficiently, with openness and transparency; building a team I could trust; having the best intentions; always aiming to exceed expectations; and understanding and using the power of word-of-mouth advertising. Word of mouth, in fact, was the very thing that had brought me to Kate's door.

If there was one thing that stuck in my East Coast craw during that time, as I'd watched and worked with other businesses, it was how often I'd witnessed—and had to accommodate—blatant, nonsensical inefficiencies. Imagine you're really hungry. You have a short lunch break, so grabbing a quick sandwich is your best option. But you have to go to one store for the bread, another for the meat, and a third for condiments. You'll also need fresh veggies, so stop by the local market. Now transfer that scenario over to the construction industry. Having to go to a different contractor or supplier for each separate aspect of a job is not only time-consuming, it's costly. It makes no sense.

Kate's request—to be able to deal with any maintenance or building needs with a single call—affirmed my belief in what the industry was lacking, and what I had to offer. It was the nudge I needed to put my dream system in motion. I couldn't have been more excited. I gave Kate with a K my biggest, most enthusiastic Bear smile.

"Kate, my dear, send me the list, and if the brothers need their feet rubbed after lunch, I'll be there."

It wouldn't take rocket science to change the industry: it was a plain old matter of organization. One of the first components in my "one-stop shop" company was a manual work-order management system:

a client would tell us in a single call what their needs were, and we would sort, separate, and manage the jobs from there. This approach was unheard of in the industry. It felt, at the front end, cumbersome. But I knew it would save time, money, and staffing, and it would get the job done quicker. And the simplicity it offered to clients was what people wanted—it was exactly why I'd gotten the call from Kate with a K.

For so long, I'd shaken my head at how no one seemed to notice the inefficiencies in the trades—or to recognize the huge potential that reversing these inefficiencies would unleash. Maybe the reason the status quo reigned was because to change it took plain old work: setting priorities, thinking ahead. True innovation isn't about the exciting moment when the rocket lifts off: it's about all the careful, detailed, even tedious work that makes liftoff possible.

My new way of doing business had unlimited potential, but I knew I'd need a company name—one that I could build up as a "brand." My first crack at it was pretty simple: "All-in-One." That obviously covered the gist of what I was up to. But it had the appeal of a bowl of three-day-old cold cream of wheat with no sugar added. Blech.

One night, I was out for dinner with a friend in New Brunswick, where I'd travelled with my team for a job. She was curious and asked me to explain what my business was all about. I told her we were doing commercial cleaning jobs, lighting, plumbing, floor replacements, facade work, and everything in between. I told her, excitedly, about my "one phone call" principle.

"So, you're kind of like a fresh face in the industry," she said.

She was right. "Fresh" might just fit a female in a male-dominated industry, someone with no formal education in the fields of construction *or* business management who was hell-bent on doing things differently. A fresh approach to an age-old industry.

I laughed. "I'm kind of the fresh-ass everything."

My friend laughed, too, and told me she was convinced I was going to be a millionaire by the time I was thirty. I quite liked the way she was thinking. But time would tell. In the meantime, we raised our glasses and hashed through some potential company names.

Soon after that inspiring conversation, Freshco was born. In 1995, at the ripe old age of twenty, I initiated the first full-service, 24/7, on-call retail maintenance company in the country. I was off-the-charts pumped. Holy shit, Batman. I was actually doing this.

It was going to take time, not just to build up clientele but also to reset their expectations to the level of service we could provide. The industry had been so inefficient for so long, I sometimes felt like shaking people awake, telling them, "You should expect better. You deserve better!"

In Freshco's early days we took on a job for a Gap location in a Halifax shopping centre. The directive was clear enough: "Mandy, go out back and realign all our clothing holders and lay new VCT. We want new clothing bins." (For those who are interested, VCT stands for "vinyl composition tile.") They sent drawings and everything else I needed to get started.

The manager met me at the front door of the shop and led me into the back. "We were told this job would take two weeks of over-nights," she said.

I wasn't sure I'd heard her correctly. Two weeks for this job? What was everyone smoking? I told her, to her surprise, that we'd have it completed in three nights. And we did.

The next thing you know, my phone rang, showing a Toronto

number. My dealings with folks from Toronto had, to this point, been pretty much nonexistent. A man was on the line, shouting at me and loving on me at the same time.

It was the Gap's facilitator from Toronto. The manager had emailed him photos of the job. Everything worked, it was all operating perfectly, it all looked great. He didn't believe it until he saw the photos. He could not understand how we'd done this job in three nights.

"Who are you?" he shouted at me. "And why the hell are you over there?"

"On the East Coast, you mean?" I asked.

"Yes! I have two stores there, and I've got over a hundred here. I need you to come to Toronto."

This man was serious. I hadn't thought about expanding outside Eastern Canada, but all at once I realized I could. Starting in Toronto, the biggest consumer hub in Canada, I could move anywhere and set up the exact same structure and strategy. Having a base in Toronto would make it possible to expand further west. Quebec would be tricky, but I never feared it. (To this day, my French is shit. But once you understand the lay of the land there, and respect it, you can get along just fine.)

Now, more than twenty-five years later, Freshco (not the grocery store!—more on that later) covers all of Canada, the eastern United States, and beyond. Freshco.ca has become an award-winning boutique facilities firm, specializing in multi-site maintenance and project construction. Every day brings further evidence that, all those years ago, young as I was, I was so right: there was a glaring gap in the industry, and I'd figured out how to fill it.

Back when I'd gotten that call from Kate with a K, to help her keep things running smoothly at the very heart of coolness in Halifax culture—to tweak the HVAC, de-squeak the elevators, and shine the windows at Salter Street Films—I felt like I'd hit the ball out of the park. Now I understood there was no reason I couldn't go even further and take on major clients beyond my own backyard. I was learning fast, and the business was building.

But not too fast. One client—one phone call—at a time.

9

BE THE SMART-ASS BLUE COLLAR LESBIAN IN THE BOARDROOM— IF THAT'S THE REAL YOU

The silence stretched. Expressionless faces. Not a smirk or twinkle to be found. They were still taking it in. That was all.

Right?

Had I hit the mark, or missed it by a mile?

We're back in San Francisco now, people. I've just walked scared shitless into the boardroom in my freshly stapled, butt-soaked Reitmans pants.

And what have I done? What have I said that's sucked all the air out the room? Oh, right.

The giant in charge, Francisco, had told me I came highly recommended. He was interested in what I had to say. I'd replied—of course, what else would I say?—"Well, it's a good thing, because Canadian lesbians don't travel to San Francisco all dressed up like this for just any guys."

What had I been thinking? I'd been thinking I'd warm these guys up. Break through their slick armour. Make them laugh, open their eyes and see not just another pitch in front of them, but me—Mandy Rennehan. The person behind that pitch.

The call that had sent me hurtling across the continent in a jet and into the Gap's west coast headquarters had come as a result of my expansion to Toronto. I *had* built a successful new retail maintenance program for Gap's Ontario stores, after all. (It was only their biggest market in Canada.) After sewing that up, I'd gone to the manager who'd lured me there and said, "What do you think about me taking over Canada?" That was way beyond his pay grade, he'd told me. "You need to go to San Francisco and talk to the bigwigs." Because of the work I was doing, he put my name before them. He recommended me.

Making my pitch to the Gap was—I knew it even then—one of the most important moments of my life. A contract this size had the potential to make my business. But the measly seven-minute window I'd been allotted was ticking away.

Suddenly, Francisco, the giant in charge, broke into a high-pitched, jovial laugh. Soon the whole room was laughing—except me. Now that the laughter I'd hoped for was in full swing, I couldn't read it. Were they laughing *with* me, or about to laugh me out of the room?

Finally, Francisco spoke. "You know what? You're funny. I love that. And apparently you're also very smart. So let's have it."

I launched into my pitch—my first top-drawer corporate pitch— and it quickly became clear that the trades were not my only art. I told those executives I could change the face of Gap's retail business in Canada. The idea was to make their retail maintenance program way more store-centric. It would mean less work on the store's part and a longer lifespan for the commercial space, and it would give them way more bang for their buck. Even better, it was simple—so simple, it was extraordinary that I was the first to pitch them this way. Following the logic I'd used in that early RFP with Canada Post, I said, "It's like this. Instead of getting your car painted once a year, we'll wash and polish it four times a year. It'll last longer, and, in the long run, cost you less."

It was an innovative approach to maintenance, one they'd never heard. The handful of minutes Boy Wonder had allotted me stretched to an hour. They were interested. They were with me. Francisco's manner was kind and warm, but it was clear that he was also a sharp, critical thinker. He was looking for an authentic presentation. His whole persona was: *I'm friendly, but if you're feeding me a line of shit, I'm going to very nicely show you the door.* But because I'd already piloted my method on Gap's Ontario stores, there was nothing he asked me that I couldn't answer. During my pitch, I could sense the mutual respect rising to fill the space between us. And his growing confidence in me filtered around the table, where his colleagues sat listening. I could feel it happen: they were coming onboard. I might actually have a hope in hell of winning this enormous contract.

But I had a weak spot: I was self-financed, so didn't have the money or a large enough team to do everything they wanted done all at once. I'd need to ramp my operations up, and that wouldn't happen overnight. I was determined to be upfront about this. Better to lower expectations and then, with sound management, exceed them, than the other way around.

"I can do this," I said. "But I'll need time. It's going to take two years to complete, but it'll be done right."

Then I held my breath.

"It's not usually an option for us," Francisco said. "But you know what, Mandy? We trust you, and we'll allow it."

I started to breathe again. I had just landed—for fucking real—a multi-million-dollar contract to take over maintenance of all Canadian Gap stores.

Well over a decade had passed and so much had happened since my days as a ten-year-old kayak-netting entrepreneur. I'd obviously learned tons about business. But my basic bottom-line way of operating hadn't changed. Even though I was unsure how things would pan out, and even if the world was not exactly co-operating—I had a child's curfew and a heavy load uphill by bicycle to contend with on the one hand; cheap clothes and zero experience with corporate America on the other—I did what I thought needed doing, and said what I thought needed saying. Even terrified as all get out, I trusted myself, followed my instincts, and barrelled ahead.

After settling the details, Francisco sent his boys out of the room, looked me straight in the eyes, and said, "You know what, Mandy? It seems that we're both outsiders. I'm from Chile, and God knows where you're from. More time together is definitely in order. Why don't we take my very small San Francisco car out to get a coffee?"

Thirty seconds later, my stapled pants, my four-million-dollar contract, my new, taller-than-the-Friendly Giant friend and I walked back out through what had, an hour before, been the two most intimidating doors I'd ever encountered.

The immensity of what had just happened was, I gotta say, a bit uncomfortable in the fit department. It's like that first Armani blazer you put on. You know it's freaking fabulous. It fits perfectly. You're going to wear it like you were born with it. But that doesn't mean it's not a bit weird at first. It takes some getting used to.

The deal, the work, the whole package was beyond exciting. But what was just as important was the bond that was beginning to form between Francisco and me. Building relationships and trust is of the utmost importance. It provides a strong foundation for moving forward. I'd come to like and respect Francisco in a very short amount of time. I was comfortable in his presence. And now, to forge the friendship further, we were heading out for that coffee. (Newfoundland was still there, of course. I had to rely on her patience; we reconnected later.)

We took the elevator to the garage and got into Francisco's black Saab convertible. He had the top up, and when he got in, his head hit the damn roof.

"My son," I said, "you need yourself a truck for the size of you."

He smiled. "That would be very un-San Francisco-like, Mandy. So my wife tells me."

"Fair enough. Now what do you think? Are we gonna go to Starbucks and get a caramel macchiato?" *That sounded West Coast*, I thought.

His answer was a firm, "No." He told me that one of the guys behind Starbucks had started another, better, coffee shop. "P-E-E-T-S," he spelled out for me. Peet's. "Mandy, we're going for some real coffee here in San Francisco."

Off we went, looking pretty fly, if I must say so myself. We chatted about where he came from, and where I'd grown up, and life in general. The conversation was easy and flowed steadily.

"Mandy, do you know why I've stuffed you into my car and taken you out for coffee?"

My little "I'm-not-gonna-answer" grin appeared, as I waited for him to answer his own question.

"Because, not only are you going to make me look good in my job, but I trust you. More importantly, I like you."

He had just spoken my language.

I've never accepted or condoned discrimination of any kind. I believe in the human spirit, regardless of a person's gender, religion, heritage, age, colour. I'm thankful for the many men—I say "men" because I've encountered and dealt with so many in the trades, especially early on—who have come into my life and let me be exactly who I am, without question or judgment. Francisco knew I was female, but that's not the lens he chose to view me through. He didn't see me as being gay. He didn't see me as Canadian. Oh, he knew I was all those things. But he saw someone in front of him with not a bit of pretence—the real deal.

Because I'd shown him my personality, because I didn't pretend, the trust was built. We can't be afraid to be our true selves. In fact, we need to embrace who we are. Anything else is extremely exhausting. Who wants to run a business—or live, for that matter—like that, tiring themselves out by trying, every day, to put on a face that doesn't fit? Too many do, though, because they think that's what's expected, and that's what will work.

I know from experience: they're wrong. People crave "real" because it's so damn rare. "Real" is what netted me a multi-million-dollar contract in my twenties. "Real," I'd always suspected, and now knew for certain, would catapult me forward in this industry. But it's about more than that. When I'm just being me, it gives those around me permission to do the same. In a world of stiff white collars, that matters.

Over coffee, Francisco paid me the ultimate compliment. "You know, there are beautiful places in this city to eat, but I'd love for you to come to my home tonight, for dinner. I'd love for my wife to meet you."

Unfortunately, I couldn't accept. Newfoundland and I were booked on a flight home that night. If that had happened today, I'd change reservations in a flash. But such a luxury wasn't an option back then, because building a business means not wasting a single penny. Still, there are moments in life when you're just humbled beyond words. Bringing someone you've just met home to meet the family is a big deal in my books, and I was honoured to be asked. I knew this was as promising a start as I could get—for this contract, and this relationship.

Our flight home was way less fraught. There was no mad dash to buy new clothes before checking in at the airport. I'd managed to avoid a seatmate with toxic breath. No longer psyching myself up for the most important meeting of my life so far, I was able to eat.

The pilot made a smooth landing and we were safely back on Nova Scotia soil. I was in my early twenties, and with all this chubby Maritime Bear had experienced in the past two days, I readied myself. Because life was about to hit warp speed.

I was one hundred percent right about the significance of landing that contract. Scaling up to manage maintenance for Gap stores across Canada meant learning the lay of the land—the very different land— in each part of the country. No matter where I showed up, someone would inevitably say, with a smile, "You must be an East Coaster." I realized just how much respect the rest of Canada had for us, and I made sure I gave them our East Coast best.

But that was the *only* consistency province to province. Because in this blessed nation we call home, every province features not just its own culture and geography, but also its own set of building codes and regulations. It wasn't just a matter of following them: I had to become an expert on them all. Once you crossed a provincial border, anything and everything could change: your contacts, your costs, the shipping regulations. It was my job to navigate all that. The learning curve was challenging—but satisfying.

It also opened more doors: door after door after door. Freshco has since served a wide variety of retail giants: Anthropologie, Apple, lululemon, Banana Republic, Sephora, Restoration Hardware, Nike, Under Armour, Tiffany & Co, Home Depot, Tesla, and many more: I know, a pretty mediocre client list, right? Ha! There was a time when I could only dream about shopping in most of these companies' stores, let alone have them on my client roster. So I'm humbled and thankful every time we sign a new contract. And I haven't, not for one second, forgotten the moment I walked into that boardroom in San Francisco—the moment I made those executives laugh.

Every one of these remarkable businesses I just listed, and the many others that Freshco works with, has renewed, renovated, and rebranded with our help. They also, on occasion, have issues with lighting, flooring, and toilet "deposits" not going down in the manner intended. It may not all be glamorous, but whatever they're dealing with, they turn to us—that single phone call—and know we'll sort it out.

While the world is sleeping, the Freshco team comes in, in stealth mode, works through the night, and leaves that retail space in top condition. We are sometimes fondly referred to as a company's chief nutritionist and favourite plastic surgeon, all-in-one package. Daily, millions of shoppers experience the changes Freshco makes, and the maintenance jobs we keep up with, and they never give their surroundings a second thought. We like it that way.

The Gap remains a Freshco client to this day. The new king on the Gap throne, who I've worked with for the past ten years, will text me when he needs to: "Lobster, I need your eyes on this one."

And he knows I'll jump as quickly as I did twenty-five years ago.

10

GUARD YOUR "WOOD WHISPERER" CRED WITH YOUR LIFE

I was a woman in her twenties from faraway Nova Scotia, in a storefront in Santa Rosa, California, staring at a wood floor with a bunch of sixty-year-old men. The floor had been recently laid, but it showed signs of cupping: the boards were taking on a swell. When you see this effect, it's like the wood is screaming. It doesn't like the conditions it's in *at all*.

The wood in question was eucalyptus, an exotic wood from South Africa, often seen as a sustainable material because the trees are fast growing. The new floor wasn't living up to the CSI team's hopes. Yes, that's right: this company was known as the crime scene investigators of flooring, with a reputation for getting to the bottom of any problem with any kind of wood. Its client wanted an entire floor of this exotic wood installed in a building on the Magnificent Mile, Chicago's premier commercial district.

These guys could have been my great-uncles. They'd worked in this field for what seemed (to me) like a lifetime. But I could only shake my head over the hope they were placing in this eucalyptus floor. I'd travelled from the cold, damp environment of Eastern Canada to sunny California. Where I came from, we wore parkas and raincoats ten months out of the year. I understood the vast difference between Chicago and California, and I understood that the plan in question, to lay South African wood in a high-end Windy City retail space, was pure folly.

One of any retailer's biggest assets is its flooring, and if anyone could make sure that asset was protected, it was this Bear. I was still in my early twenties, but my reputation for understanding wood products of every kind—seeded after I'd taken over that fancy flooring job in that luxury Halifax home and surprised the client with the quality of my work—had earned me the nickname "The Wood Whisperer."

My love for wood had been sparked back in the days of my log cabin enterprise, at the ripe old age of twelve. Chopping down trees in the woods with the boys, shaving the bark, and piling logs into walls, I'd come to appreciate the problem with spruce—Nova Scotia's ubiquitous softwood. It's dirty, it bends, it leaks a shitload of sticky sap. Whereas a birch tree, though harder to cut down, could hold a lot more weight. And no sap issues. And I saw that pine, though also soft, was beautiful. I started to teach myself the difference among species and the characteristics of each kind of wood.

As I came to work with wood professionally—I laid wood floors, I cleaned them, refinished them—I quickly got to know what thickness you'd need for which purpose, which woods were durable in which climates, and the importance (an importance way too often overlooked) of properly acclimatizing wood to its new environment.

Wood is very similar to humans. When the sun comes up, we're alive. When the cold comes in, we want to shrivel up and die. When you're bringing it from a warehouse that was 38°C to a store that's only 25°C, that's like somebody from the jungle coming to Canada in February. They're like, "Holy shit, what just happened?" You don't want to put that hardwood in place while it's still trying to figure out if this is where it wants to live. You bring it into the store, and you let it sit. And if you lay wood on a surface that's cold and has moisture coming up through it, it's constantly going to contract, because it doesn't like that.

I learned that if you wanted the rough warehouse look, you wanted pine—you wanted people to beat the shit out of it with their shoes. I learned that walnut is stunning, but temperamental: it doesn't like heat or cold, and there's no undoing the damage from a scratch. I learned the value of a good Canadian maple—extremely hard, durable, and, with water-based stains (which were just making headway when I was starting out), easily transformed to resemble a more expensive exotic wood, such as mahogany.

I built maintenance programs for different hardwoods in different environments. I could tell a client *this* floor, in *this* city, in *this* store, on *this* street needs to be screened and recoated four times a year, or you're going to lose it. That same floor indoors, in a mall, in a smaller town with less foot traffic, will need a whole lot less love and attention to last.

So while I was a bit surprised that my credibility was widespread enough that I'd been called to consult on this problem with the eucalyptus floors, I was more than confident of what I had to offer. There we all were: a small fortune's worth of this beautiful wood, three CSIs, a couple of consultants for good measure, and the Canadian Wood Whisperer, trying to figure out what the problem was, and—these guys all still hoped—how to make this wood product work in Chicago.

Eucalyptus is one of the most beautiful species of wood on this earth, but to bring its best self to light, as with a person, you must first understand it. The thing to know about eucalyptus, especially in relation to the present case, was that it's a finicky wood, one that doesn't adapt well to unfamiliar climates.

I was sure, looking at this floor, that the wood hadn't been properly acclimatized before the planks were laid. It looked like the installers hadn't used a vapour barrier either. As for replicating the same eucalyptus floor in a retail space a few blocks from the shore of Lake Michigan? I was blunt. "This is never gonna work in Chicago," I told them. "Not on a street-level store. Never."

Problem number one, I explained: the variability of climate in Chicago, where temperatures can range from over 30 degrees (that's Celsius, folks) in summer, with a humidex in the 40s, to minus 25°C (with a wind chill of minus 30°C or colder) in the winter. Chicago is on Lake Michigan, adding to the temperature ups and downs and the moisture in the air.

The other issue was road salt. This floor, I told them, would not stand up to the winters in a city where salt is tracked in off the streets all day, every day. If the stains were not cleaned quickly, a floor made of eucalyptus would suffer serious damage in short order. It didn't have the abrasion value. It would pit. And I'd bet my bottom dollar that no business was going to hire someone with a mop to clean up after every person tracking through. I believe eucalyptus was chosen for its hardness and its density: in a tropical setting, it's a superstar. But to lay it at street level in a winter climate? It's going to be temperamental, it's going to cup, you're not going to be happy with the outcome.

The team members listening to me seemed to tilt their heads in a way that suggested they didn't understand what I was saying.

"The wood is going to lift," I told them, slowly and pointedly. I hoped that was clear enough to sink in.

"That's not what the manufacturer said," someone protested.

"We'll acclimatize it in the store," another guy added.

I could tell these poor souls were hoping beyond hope that their arguments would somehow translate to the truth, and all would be well with this project. We all knew there was a lot at stake here: money and time, for a start. But reputations were at stake as well. And which, when all is said and done, do *you* think is most valuable? For me, there was no contest. I wasn't going to recommend laying a floor for a high-end Magnificent Mile retailer that was inappropriate for the location and bound to deteriorate on warp speed.

We could have argued in circles all day. But I'm not one to waste time, so it was time for me to pull out the "Will this convince you?" card.

"Okay, boys, if the manufacturer will provide the wood, I'll lay the floor for free. I'll have someone go in each week and send you before-and-after pictures. Even with mechanical controls in place, the shift in climate is going to take its toll on these floors."

Call me in but don't trust me? I was just getting started in this business, and that shit was already getting old. I needed to show this retailer that I knew my stuff. I would prove to them, if this floor went down, that these nincompoops had no idea what they were talking about when it came to the other side of the earth—where there's weather, real weather. They'd brought me in for a second opinion, so clearly they already had their doubts.

But the offer I'd just made was rash. I didn't have the fucking money to back myself up. It would cost eighty thousand dollars to lay one of those floors. I thought, *If they actually take me up on this offer, and I'm wrong, holy shit, I'm screwed without a condom.*

I must have had my best poker face on, because they said no, they'd pay me to lay the floor—but only the first section to start. I would test it and send before-and-after photos, as we'd discussed. This was a solution I could live with. I thanked my lucky stars.

And I was proven right. Within three months of being laid, the floors were a dog's breakfast. The CSI team respectfully admitted defeat, thankful in the end for the clarity they could bring to their client: solid proof that this wood would not work in this environment. I, meanwhile, came away with a new nickname, courtesy of the CSI guys: The Northern Wind. Because, as they put it, I had basically ripped their backbones out and beat 'em with them.

It became a standing but friendly joke among us, though for me it was more, because I had earned a deeper level of respect from my colleagues. The days of having to prove myself were coming to an end. That was more important to me than anything I might have earned on this particular job. There is nothing like word of mouth to build a business. And word of mouth rests on reputation.

My reputation as the Wood Whisperer was intact.

11

FOLLOW YOUR HEART—RIGHT INTO THE EMOTIONAL LAND OF HOME RENOS

O n the forty-second day of the six-week period we had promised to finish dramatically transforming their home, exactly to the hour, the Leaps walked in the front door.

My team and I were used to the different ways people react to their completed home renovations: tears, gasps, bulging eyes, exclamations of "Oh my God," "WTF," and "Wow." What happened with Veronica Leap was a new one, even for me. She. Said. Nothing.

I didn't try to force a conversation. Instead, we hugged. Her husband, Rob, said, with a wink, "I'll call you later."

I was confident in the work we'd done. I left smiling. When we chatted later that day, Rob said, "Mandy, I've been married to this woman for more than twenty-five years, and I have never seen her speechless." He told me to let her settle into the space. She would touch base soon. As for himself, he assured me, "I'm absolutely thrilled."

I believed in the quality of our work. The house was stunning. But I was a little shaky, I'll admit.

What could I do? I waited.

Come closer. I want to introduce you to my two competing loves. One is pleasing, practical, relatively cool, and completely functional. The other is beautiful, emotional, and inviting, with soft lines and endless possibilities. Meet commercial and residential. Both have been very good to me. My commercial business may not cause me to fall into an emotional heap, but I do love it, in part because I know it's the means to the other: my residential business, where I'm in my element, a baby bear playing in a stream of salmon.

I don't know where I picked up the knack for residential, but I have it, and it shows. In every home I've bought, remade, and sold (at last count, twenty-five). With every house I flipped, I saved my money and lived with less so I could buy another home. I handpicked each person on my team. And I apply all the thousands of lessons I've learned buying and remaking houses to each and every residential project I take on. Imagine waking up every day in an ideal environment, one that suits you perfectly, where you enjoy your morning coffee smack dab in the utopia you used to encounter only on movie screens, or in magazines with names like *Dream Home Quarterly*. Imagine looking around with a goofy grin as you realize "This is mine." Imagine sipping a glass of wine under a nineteenth-century chandelier, dimmed to half-light. (Holy Hannah, it's getting hot in here!) It's your space, and, within it, you are safe, at peace, comfortable. That I can create a living space that induces a warm glow of contentment in its owners makes me happier than I can say.

I spend big helpings of time with my residential clients, learning who they are, what they need, and what they want. My reputation for giving them exactly what they've hoped for, with no scrimping and the highest-quality work, means people will wait years—yes, *years*—for me to renovate their homes.

But here's the deal: after we conduct very thorough consultations with our clients, their renovations have to be done on my terms—and my terms alone. I tell each of them, "This is my price. Now, you need to leave. And I do not want to hear from you until I'm done."

"But …"

That's the first word I always hear.

"Nope! My terms. Take it or leave it."

The looks I get are hilarious. Try telling a control freak to get out, and stay out, until my team is finished—and, no, you cannot have a say beyond the consultations that have already taken place.

You have to trust me, my sweet.

To make sure they know I believe in what I can do for them, I'll sweeten the deal by telling them if they're not 150 percent satisfied with the design and function and everything else my team does, then they won't have to pay me. That's how damn confident I am in the job I do. And I have never once had an issue.

I don't adopt this policy to send my clients—or me—into fits of anxiety. It's practical. This Bear isn't afraid of a fight, but a fight is what you get if you have too many people trying to run the show. Far too often, I've seen four or more people trying to be the boss on a project. The designer who doesn't understand construction or the costs of making significant changes in an existing home tells everyone where the toilet should be, which is always across the room (heaven forbid a designer keep anything in its place). The owner isn't sure, but wants to trust the designer. The plumber is trying to tell you what it'll take workwise. The general contractor is figuring out how to get the work done with the changes. "Move the toilet" is *never* simple, and a fight will follow, with everyone trying to be heard.

So, we need some facts.

Facts, you ask?

Yes. Here's one, for a start: moving a toilet can add ten thousand dollars or more to the price of a bathroom renovation. Think about it. If you move the damn thing halfway across the house, you'll have to cut open the ceiling below and maybe even cut through a second ceiling, further down. Oh, and don't forget floor joists, venting, and more. And the worst thing? No one tells the owners that it's going to cost them ten thousand dollars more to take a shit in a new place versus the old.

When I do a residential reno, I make it easy—for the owners as well as for me and my team. How do I do this? All-in-one. I'm not just a general contractor. I'm the designer. I'm the blueprint. I'm the builder. I've always stockpiled what's needed in my warehouses, and my commercial business sources everything. On top of all that, I make damn sure to tell the owners—who, incidentally, are paying the bills—that the cost will vary, depending on what changes are made. Stick with the plan, people, and save yourselves a winter-in-Florida's worth of money.

The problem is, people are afraid to say what they are thinking. Is the change in design a good idea? Bad idea? What are the costs? How much more time will it take? In my world, we need to find a place where the project is on budget and on time, there are no surprises, and the owners get exactly what they want and need.

Giving people a stunning product, more than they expected or even hoped for, is actually easy, and it never has to cost them an arm and a leg—or any other body part.

You see, what folks often don't understand is that the cost of labour is not based on the quality of the product. If you pick out tiles priced at $2.13 per square foot, it'll cost the same amount of money to lay them as it will to lay tiles that cost twenty-eight dollars per square foot. Keeping those prices in mind, in a hundred-thousand-dollar renovation or new construction, you'll save maybe ten thousand dollars, or 10 percent, going with cheap-ass, builder-grade, we-look-like-we-came-from-the-eighties tiles, because, again, the labour costs don't change. I help my clients understand that for a modest additional cost, they can have a timeless, sexy home that wows everyone who steps into it. Bam!

The same please-do-it-right premise applies to heating and cooling systems. My partner, Annie, and I were renting a home while she waited for me to build our own. For the love of Pete, I could not understand, given the amount of money I dished out for that beautiful new space, why we were freezing in the winter and couldn't breathe in the summer.

But let me take a stab at why that heating and cooling system was out of whack. It was a big house, and it needed a split system. But a general contractor who thinks they are doing you a favour by giving you the cheapest, most boring, missionary-style design decides to put in one system that is now responsible for pumping hot *or* cold air uphill from 40 feet away, all the way to where my head is lying on what *would* be my comfy bed if I wasn't freezing my ass off (or sweating buckets). In a new house. Why would anyone do that? The system isn't made to cool or heat at those distances any more than the person who cuts my hair is qualified to service my car. For an extra ten thousand dollars—not so big a price tag on a million-dollar home—the system could have been perfect. But, no, someone had to cheap out. Would you pay an extra ten thousand dollars (amortized over thirty years, that's $333 per year) to make sure you would be comfortable no matter the season? Damn right you would. But if you're not given your options, you don't know the difference.

Unless my team is doing the work. Just saying.

I sound pretty confident, don't I? Sure of the service I provide and the skill and professionalism of my team.

Remember the Leaps? They'd returned to their home, which I'd remade from top to bottom after sending them away with my most convincing Bear promises and my usual home-reno order: to leave, and leave everything to me. Six weeks later, Veronica had walked into her renovated home, looked around, and not said a word. Not. A. Single. Word.

Two days had passed, and I still hadn't heard from her.

Let's back up.

At the turn of the century (damn, that makes me feel old), in Oakville, Ontario (the Beverly Hills of Canada), a community was being designed with the promise of above-standard luxury and quality. The Leaps were one of the families who eagerly moved into this new community. Sara, my partner at that time, was a nutritionist and personal trainer. She had a studio in our Oakville house, and one of her clients was Veronica Leap, a leading professional in the humanitarian and nonprofit sector. One day, when I was working from home, Veronica came over to, as I like to put it, get the shit kicked out of her. When she emerged from her session, she said,

"God, I love this woman, but, man, does she have two faces." I knew what she meant about Sara: really sweet, while simultaneously (as a consummate professional) kicking your ass. I said to Veronica, "Listen, I'm cranking a bottle of wine." She joined me, and we launched into a hearty conversation about business, ethics, charities, and the not-for-profit world. We hit it off. We became friends.

A few years later, when she and her husband wanted to fully renovate their "Beverly Hills" home, she reached out to me. "Bear, I know you're expensive, but Roy and I can't go through another damn nightmare. When we bought our home, the first renovations just about killed us."

My ears pricked up. First renovations? The house was only a little over a dozen years old, and they were already in need of round two? Please, please, please don't tell me they didn't get what they'd paid for, and what they were promised.

That was exactly the case. Like far too many homes I walk through, theirs had come all nicely wrapped in bullshit promises of quality that ended up being bare-ass lies: substandard finishes, low-quality materials, and just poor basic design—the house lacked functionality of space, for a start.

I have the ability, partly from my vast trades experience and partly from sheer instinct, to draw out a renovation in my mind. I can engineer it with someone I trust, design it, and build it. Normally I sit with clients long enough to understand who they are and where they're at right now. What means something to them in terms of art and photography? What, functionally, don't they like about their house? Are they planning to retire there? If so, does the house have accessibility issues we should address? Do they ever foresee a kid moving back in? Do they have lots of visitors? Is it important to them—as it damn well is to me—that they don't have to share a washroom with someone else?

Beyond all that, I ask them, "What would make you wake up and say to yourself, *I'm not leaving the house this weekend?*" Usually they'll look at each other. They can't answer that one. I'll say, "Here's twenty bucks. Go have two cold beers, two cheap glasses of wine, then come back and tell me." A lot of times, it comes down to: We want to upgrade our fireplace. We want to make sure our TV is set up in a place where we can cuddle. We want to have mood lighting. Someone will want carpet on the stairs so their feet won't get cold. It's a spiral effect. They'll come back with two things, and by the end of the week they'll have given me twenty. I'm asking them to think differently. To look at the resale value, but also the comfort in their home.

This is where my experience comes in. I'll come back and say, I'm giving you eight of these items on your wish list. The other twelve are preposterous, and you don't have the money. These eight, though, will serve you if you stay here. And, if you sell your house, they'll serve someone else as well. These are what we call "shared function." Double wall ovens are going to be a function most people will enjoy. So is a basement with a walkout and a separate nanny suite. But a basement with a bowling lane? Not a shared function. Pools are not a shared function. But a beautiful, landscaped backyard with a stone or wood deck? Yes. Jack-and-Jill washrooms for the kids, with maple leaf tiles or Barbie? Your kids are going to outgrow that in three or four years. It'll be a huge renovation to remove. If you want to make them cute, do it with paint.

And so on.

As for Veronica and her husband, I knew this couple well enough to appreciate what would fix the mistakes in their home and make it what they'd hoped it would be from the start. We knew they loved to entertain, and that a space for their grandkids that was bright and beautiful was important. We knew that Veronica's husband, an artist, came alive when he talked about his paintings: he had a firecracker in his eye. We also knew (because he told us) that he wanted a sauna. I set out the plan, the cost, and my usual terms: essentially, leave everything to me.

For Veronica, a successful executive, handing over the reins was about as comfortable as trying to brush the back of a wild stallion. "Bear," she said, "this is the hardest thing I've ever been tasked with. And the price is higher than I budgeted—"

Before she could finish her thought, I stopped her. "Sweetie, it's like this: You've waited over eighteen months for me to take on this project. It will be done in six weeks and not a day longer. And if you don't love it, you don't pay. But I guarantee you will double your money on the open market with the work I'm going to complete."

She gave me her beautiful Veronica smile and said, "I don't know about that, but what the hell? I trust myself to trust you!"

One month later we started gutting this luxury (my arse) home. I love nothing more than aggravating people I adore, so I started sending random photos of tile, light fixtures, various fabrics—just to put Veronica over the edge with curiosity. But she knew the rules: no peeking in the dead of night when my team wasn't there. Otherwise, this panda turned grizzly would become her new nightmare.

One of the most frustrating parts of doing residential work in geographic areas where we need to bring on trade partners who haven't worked with us before is that they'll assume I'm just the general contractor, not also the designer and decorator. This isn't their fault; it's what they're used to. While working on the Leaps' place, I was continually being questioned about why I was laying hardwood in a particular pattern or why the old pot lights were being pulled back, or why was I running an extra water line when there was already one there.

What I started to realize was that the professionals I needed for manual labour didn't have the faintest clue about design or function for a different lifestyle. They also couldn't envision what the finished product could be if I made it my mission to turn these people from questioning skeptics into fans.

I also made adjustments as necessary. We always did everything in our power to hire the best people for the job, but that didn't make them Mandys. Five weeks in, we fired our plumber because he didn't make the job a priority. We also let apprentices with bad attitudes go, the ones who thought they didn't have to do simple finish work.

Even with those bumps, things came together, as they usually did. In a family room with 20-foot ceilings, we did away with the shitty builder-grade fan and pot lights. We hung a 4 x 12 stainless steel mirror that weighed 900 pounds over a mantle that had been underused. Then we added two 25-inch grey linen Cicero barrel pendants on either side; finished custom transoms over what had been boring standard doors; and a chevron-feature wall with a hint-of-Versailles parquet border. (Shit, turn up the AC—it's getting *hot*.)

It took strategy and logistics—and hard work. We had to get staging in there, the ceilings were so high. But we transformed that room into a haven—a functional, inviting, beautiful haven. A room they'd never want to leave.

In the kitchen, their expensive cabinetry (even the handles and knobs), though beautiful, had outgrown the backsplash and countertops. This is like having a dirty Lamborghini: you're not showing your treasure at its best. We brought the cabinetry and its "jewellery" in sync.

We transformed the basement, which had been unfinished, into a bright, luxury living space that featured the sauna Veronica's husband hoped for, as well as a selection of his best paintings, properly framed and on the wall, in a collage arrangement that celebrated his talent.

In the main washroom we installed 30-inch glass tiles with only an eighth-of-an-inch grout line that reflected the beautiful dolce vita marble on the countertops and shower sills. We laid 8-inch white-maple planked flooring with an antique walnut finish, and added a rare piece of dazzling Brazilian Albinus granite that I purchased from the only person in the city who had any at that time. (That poor excuse for a human should have been shot in the ankle with a paint gun and pissed on for how he conducted himself during that transaction. Dealing with assholes is generally a no-go in my books, but I will go to great lengths for the benefit of my clients, and this was one such instance.)

We'd outdone ourselves. It was stupendous. But there we were, two days after the big reveal, and I was still waiting to hear from Veronica.

Finally, my phone rang. It was Veronica. I picked up, smiling, to prove to myself all would be well.

"Bear," she said.

And, of course, there was a pause. I waited. I had no choice.

"I had no idea a space like this could exist. It didn't just take my words away. It took my breath away."

Whew! Okay. She kept going.

"I knew I would love it," she said, "and the work would be top notch. But this! This exceeded all my expectations." Now that she was finally talking, she couldn't get the words out fast enough. "I can't believe this is our home. And you did it on time, on budget, no stress—"

This was when she started to cry.

"Thank you, thank you, thank you."

She kept going. She let me know that she and Roy would be telling everyone about me. I finally had to interrupt her.

"Oh, heck no, keep me to yourself, Veronica!" I was too busy by then building my commercial business to take on more than the odd residential job. "These days, I squeeze in only people who I really like."

The thing is this: for me and my company, a reno isn't just you gut a house, you do it up, and you're done. No. It's a commitment. The residential projects I take on are important to me, because I know my clients' hearts are involved. When things went wrong in our home growing up, it was a nightmare because my father was not a handyman. (Nor was my mother.) It was painful. *Painful*. I believe it's important that people know who they can call if they have an issue with anything from plumbing to squeaky doors. For my own clients, I have always wanted to be the person they call first because I'll make things right immediately.

Years later when we looked back at her response, I called Veronica a bitch for keeping me pacing for forty-eight hours—and we laughed until our sides split. To this day, I get random texts telling me how she loves her home and never wants to leave.

The way I feel when I read those texts? That is how you want your work to make you feel.

12

―

HONOUR YOUR BROTHER,
HONOUR YOUR LOSS

I t was Super Bowl Sunday, 2006, and I was up for some fun. In my world, this was friendly betting day. It was torment-the-shit-out-of-friends-and-family day. Even more so this year, because the Pittsburgh Steelers were up against the Seattle Seahawks.

My brother Chris was a Pittsburgh fan. I was for Seattle. Based on the regular season statistics, the Steelers were the underdogs that year, which fit. Chris always loved the underdog. In hockey, he cheered for the Islanders, who rarely made it to the playoffs. He called, and we made our usual bets, spiced with insults. This year, he and the boys had gathered at a buddy's place in Clare, half an hour from Yarmouth. They would watch the game, enjoying cold beers and a heap of snacks. But he didn't sound so great. It was as if he was going through the motions.

"How are you doing, dude?" I asked.

"I don't feel good at all," he said. "But I'm just hung over, Sis. It's nothing."

We talked for a while longer. Then I hung up and called my buddy in Newfoundland so we could place *our* yearly bets on the game. After that, we texted and taunted each other all the way through.

The Steelers won, 21–20. I lost my bet with Chris.

When my phone rang again, about three hours had passed since my call with Chris. It was Ma and Pup. Both of them, together. They were screeching and making noises I'd never heard before—that cross between crying so hard you can't breathe and screaming to the point there's a pitch to it you never forget.

When they could finally breathe and get the words out, this was what I heard: "Chris is dead."

Chris is dead.

It was incomprehensible to me.

Growing up with three brothers might, for someone looking in, seem pretty crowded. But I loved my brothers. Trev, my twin, had a personality that invited lighthearted teasing. Today he's made peace with that: it's part of his persona. Troy was the hockey star being scouted by universities, the "hunk" girls drooled over. He liked to think he was all that and a bag of chips. But he was our brother; we learned to live with it. And I know now there were issues that made him act like a jerk when we were kids. I love him to pieces today.

Like most brothers, Chris could sometimes be a dick, but at least he was consistent. He mostly had a steady, easy personality. Like me, he was a natural athlete, and I loved that we had that in common.

After leaving home at seventeen, I didn't see much of my family for a few years because I was going full tilt, building my business. I barely had time to sleep. One Friday evening the year I was twenty-one, I took the night off work, which was a rarity. I'd just purchased my first home and was seeing Clare, who'd recently been diagnosed with cancer—obviously a big fucking deal. We were taking it easy that night, just hanging out around the house.

There was a knock on the door. I was shocked when Clare told me my brother was there.

It was Chris. I hadn't seen him in what seemed like forever. He asked if we could go grab a beer. It was kind of a thrill that my big brother wanted to hang out. But I was curious. Was there a reason he'd come by?

Off we went to a local bar and grill.

"Sis, I really like Clare," he said. "You're lucky to be living your own life here."

Chris and I had never broached the gay subject or discussed any of my partners, and his obvious acceptance felt great.

He was a rural homeboy at heart. The rest of us had moved away, while he was the one who'd stayed. He wanted to fish like Pup. Or so he thought. He got married, had two children, and seemed to be happy in Yarmouth. He played cards and ball with his buds and did some other "fun" things that got him into a bit of trouble with his marriage, but he was a good guy.

Now he looked at me over our beers and blurted out, "Simone left me."

I was shocked. But at the same time, I wasn't.

"I'm just feeling sad about the way things are with my life."

I've never been one to beat around the bush. I figured Chris needed a dose of brutal honesty. And maybe even wanted one. Why else would he have knocked on *my* door that night? He knew me as well as anyone.

We had a long chat about how he had to make his kids and wife a priority.

"I know, Sis," he said.

I was way younger than Chris, but I was speaking from experience. I was in the middle of learning how to stick it out myself, how to support someone I cared about. Since that steamy, life-changing relationship with the farmer, Clare was the first woman I'd dated who I really cared about. She was in the beauty industry and twelve years older. I figured because I was an old soul that this woman was perfect for me. She had her own career, and we'd be aligned on many fronts.

Then, just four months into our relationship, she was diagnosed with cancer.

I was devastated. A flash of "what do I do next" hit me like a ton of bricks. The child in us never leaves, so I reached out to Ma. I told her about this woman I was dating, that she had two boys and one useless ex-husband who lived elsewhere.

It turned out Ma's listening ear was all I needed. To my core, I knew the right thing to do. I was terrified, but I couldn't walk away. It's in life's most desperate circumstances that either our worst, or our best, comes out. I spent the next year sticking by my partner, making sure she was comfortable, and with someone who genuinely cared about her. I took her two kids into my home. When I think about it, we were all kids. I'd barely crossed into my twenties. Keeping them busy, with things that took their minds off their situation and that made them feel needed, was really important.

That night, even though I was as independent as anyone my age could get, I still looked up to Chris, my older brother. So when he took my hand and told me, "Mandy, you're a sweetheart," it meant more to me than anything he'd ever said. Oh, he'd had a few beers, but I do think that's when we say what's closest to our hearts. He told me I was his hero for being all the things that everyone else wasn't when we were growing up. His words have stayed with me.

It was a serious talk, an important one, but that wasn't all he needed—he needed to relax, hang out, breathe. We spent the rest of the night eating, drinking beer, playing pool, and watching sports. I felt like I had in some little way helped him, but just as important, we had formed a new kind of bond, as adults.

Not long afterward, Chris got back together with Simone. He carried on with his life, and I carried on with mine.

Seven years passed, and much had changed. For one thing, Clare and I were no longer together. Once we both knew she was healthy enough to carry on with her own life, we'd parted ways—as friends. We both knew we weren't going to be lifelong soulmates. And I had turned my focus away from relationships for a while, to put all my energy into building my business.

Freshco had completely taken off. I'd moved to Ontario, and I had just relocated the Freshco head office from Toronto to Oakville, where I was living. My company was now a growing concern on a national scale.

I received a frantic call from Chris. He was reaching out to ask me for a loan. The Canada Revenue Agency seems especially to like auditing people who make their living fishing for lobster. Chris had endured the CRA's scrutiny three times, and he was struggling to catch up with back taxes and interest. But he was beside himself, as he absolutely hated taking anything from anyone.

"Sis, I didn't want to call, but I didn't know what to do. I'll work it off. I'll do whatever it takes." He was desperate.

"Chris, listen. I made a decision long ago that I would never, ever, lend money to anybody." It was one of my cardinal rules. "I have the money and I'll give it to you. If you want to work it off, that's up to you. But I'm going to give you the money with no strings attached."

Silence. Then Chris surprised me. "Sis," he said, all in a rush, "I don't want to be in fishing anymore." Then came the kicker: "I love what you do, and I want to learn a trade on dry land. I just need maybe a year and a half, two years to get caught up on my bills. And then I'd really like it if you would train me."

"I'll train you—no problem," I told him. I was happy, relieved to think that he wouldn't spend the rest of his life at sea.

About six months later, I flew to Moncton, New Brunswick, for a large job I'd taken on. Pup and Chris drove up from Yarmouth to meet me. The plan was to share a hotel room. My business was soaring, but why waste money?

Really, though, I should have known better than to share a room with Chris and his stinky-ass feet. They reeked so bad, they could cause a skunk to drop his stripes. Pup and I wrapped his feet in wet towels that night so we could breathe the air in the room. It was something my dear brother was known for—the stench of his feet. His friends called him Sludge.

In the morning, I brought Chris with me to our job sites in Moncton. We were reboothing a retail store and re-epoxying its floor. At another business, we were changing the storefront. He took it all in. He seemed keen to hear the trade tips I shared. I knew he'd fit in well in the trades, and we both had that to look forward to. Just another year or so fishing and catching up on his taxes, and we'd get him set up to change his career, and his life.

—

But a year later, before we even had the chance to start his training, was that awful Super Bowl Sunday.

Chris's friends later told Ma and Pup that Chris wasn't feeling well that day, just like I'd noticed during our phone call. He was sweating and kept making trips to the washroom. In fact, he was vomiting, because he was having a heart attack. He didn't know that's what was going on, and he was embarrassed. He locked the door. The last time he went in, his friend's cat started pacing in front of the door and meowing. That's when they knew there was something seriously wrong. Someone knocked. No response. Then they got really scared. They busted the door down.

But it was too late. He was gone.

At thirty-eight, Chris was gone. My homegrown, happy, grateful, rural older brother. Gone. A heart attack had taken him and robbed us all.

I got on the phone with Troy, who was out West, and Trev, who was in Ottawa, and got them on flights back home. It was February, and the weather was brutal. We had to pick up the boys at the airport. The weather was horrific. What was normally a three-hour drive turned into six or seven hours. We stopped halfway at a Tim Hortons and sat there for a few hours to wait for the plow to go through.

Back in Yarmouth, nobody knew what to do. It was the saddest, most awkward time I can recall. We had no coping skills, and no one to help us find any. Trev, Troy, and I couldn't look at each other, much less at our parents, and tell them it was going to be okay. It wasn't. They had just lost their first born without warning.

The "what ifs" don't ever disappear. What if someone had been educated on the signs of heart disease or heart attacks? What if there had been a defibrillator close by? Shit, we'd never even *heard* of a defib machine. Even worse, we had no idea there had been heart disease on mom's side of the family. It turned out that more than one of her uncles had died of heart disease under the age of fifty-five. No one thought about genetics back then. We just lived our lives, hoping for the best. But what if we'd known the family history? Would it have saved him?

Damn these what ifs. They wouldn't bring him back.

When Chris died, a part of me died with him. His loss threw everyone in our family into a bad place. My parents were broken. Chris had sons who were lost without him, so I did everything I could to support them and their mom. But, meanwhile, I was falling into a depression.

My company at the time was at a pivotal point. I remember telling Shadow, my right-hand woman who was holding everything together for me, that I would give her the company. Because I didn't want it.

Shadow and I used to walk around the building and clear our thoughts so employees wouldn't hear us. She said, "Bear, I'm here to do whatever you need me to do. You pulled me out of something I'll never be able to thank you for, and I'm going do the same for you."

Shadow held the line for me and stabilized what I'd built until I could get back to business, and back to being me.

The problem was, for a while, I didn't want to be "me" anymore. I was drinking more, pissed off at the world and feeling like a total failure—for what, I couldn't have said. My brother had dropped dead at thirty-eight. Would I be next? Would I last until thirty-eight? Would I lose another brother first? Were my parents going to die? The doctors tried to help me understand that what happened to Chris had been one in a million, and there was nothing anyone could have done to save him.

It didn't help to hear that.

I put on 40 pounds—40 extra pounds on a body that was already pretty solid. You can read all the books you want, see all the doctors in the world, but the only true healer is time. And I'd have to wait this one out.

The thing about Chris, the thing we all talk about today that's at least partly consoling, is that he was always himself. He was comfortable in his skin. He loved his kids, he loved his wife, he loved to drink, he worked hard. He was the epitome of simple. Uncomplicated. He never pretended to be the best hockey player or the best ballplayer: he was happy just to be on the team. He was the one who'd stayed home with Ma and Pup. (By home, I mean in the vicinity.) He was the one who had kids first. He was the one Pup would sit with and have a yarn about fishing or sports. If Pup was gone hunting, Chris would be, like, "Ma, do you want me to take you to church?" He was proud of who he was. He didn't need to be a CEO; he didn't need to go to university. He was the son and friend who everybody could relate to. Talking with him always took me to that safe place. When he died, I became the full-on parental figure in the family. I was alone.

There is no doubt in my mind that, had Chris lived, he'd be working with me today. He was so excited about learning the trades—as keen as I was to teach him and to have my brother close. Not everyone has a little sister to help them along, though, and so I wanted to do something for those who wanted to enter the trades, in remembrance of Chris.

I set up what began as the Chris Rennehan Scholarship Fund, which would provide scholarships to women entering the skilled trades. But it didn't take long to realize that both the government and trades schools were supplying scholarships. The reason so many women weren't sticking with the programs was that, though they had the funds for tuition, they didn't have much left over. We immediately changed the scholarship fund to the Chris Rennehan Foundation. This is how to make stuff that works: as you learn, you adapt—your enterprise, your charity, what-have-you—to your new-found knowledge. It was a common-sense decision because, without the basic supports, women were dropping out of the courses. The funds we grant are for the basics: bus tickets, Christmas, food. Plus, some extras. Heck, I've taught my team to work hard and play hard, so if some of that money goes to a meal out, or to a cold beer after a long, hard week, that's okay, too. The foundation has provided funds to many women that allow them to give the trades programs they're enrolled in their full attention.

Chris, who was on the verge of remaking his own life, would have loved it.

When Zellers was a thing—and a big deal in our small town, I might add—Chris got a job working at the store after school and on weekends. I thought it was pretty cool that my big brother had a real job.

We moved a couple of times when we were younger. One week, before one of these moves, we were packing up the house. Because Chris was working, Ma asked me to clean out his bureau.

Because Chris's feet stank enough to burn holes through his socks, Ma was constantly washing his socks and loading them into his sock drawer. He must have had fifty pairs of socks. I'd gone in many times to steal socks from his drawer, and every time, I'd seen a square box in the drawer, the kind of box that his asthma medication came in. I saw the same box this time, and didn't think twice about throwing it in the fireplace. It would be one less thing to move.

Later, after Chris got home from work, he asked where his stuff was. "Over there in the bag," Ma said. She pointed to a jumbled corner. The house was a maze of boxes and bags. "Mandy cleaned out your bureau."

When I think back, he looked relieved as he headed to the corner. But not for long. He searched through each bag, then he started ripping them apart in a frenzy.

"Where's the box? Where is it?" He was screaming at me now. "Mandy, where's the box?!"

"I threw it in the fireplace," I said.

He looked at me like he was going to take my head off.

"Oh my God, Mandy. I had four hundred dollars in that box. I've been saving it forever."

That was an enormous sum. I felt horrible.

When we buried Chris, I stood over his body, said a gut-wrenching good-bye, and left two things with him: a piece of my heart, and four hundred dollars in cash under his hand. Rest easy, big brother.

13

BUILD YOUR BAND OF MISFITS

Her name was Elaine, and she had a massive energy about her. She was also shorter than me, so of course I felt a Bear hug coming on.

"Who are you?" I asked.

She didn't know how to respond. So I asked again. "Who are you?"

Her face flushed with anxiety. *Okay*, I thought. *Time for another tack.*

"How much time did you set aside for this interview today?"

She had about three hours before she had to pick up her daughter. I handed her a loaded Starbucks card and asked if she would mind heading to the coffee shop down the street. I gave her my order—four long shots of decaf espresso—and told her to get herself whatever she wanted. On the way, I suggested, she could take a breath and think about what I was asking her.

She got up, left the building, and thirty minutes later we were both back in my office, hot drinks in hand, ready to start again.

"I thought about what you said," she began. "Nobody has ever asked me this question. I was thrown off. So here goes." She was born in Niagara Falls. She had three younger siblings. She was the daughter of a welder and a schoolteacher. Her sister had a rare leukemia growing up. "So I spent a lot of my high school years helping my parents care for her."

I was listening intently. She told me she used to get really drunk at parties because she needed the escape, but that she hadn't touched booze for quite a while. She laughed at herself over that. "I volunteer weekly at the cancer unit that helped my sister. My friends would say I have a dry sense of humour. Oh, and I love cats! I aspire to be a role model for my two younger sisters. I didn't want to go to university even though my parents wanted me to."

I inwardly smiled at that one.

She was a hands-on person who could not stand having nothing to do. "If I can't accomplish at least one thing a week that means something, I am not satisfied. And being late, or somebody else being late, is a huge issue for me. My favourite drink is a London fog, one pump." She grinned at her cup. "I love potatoes, any style. Yum."

We stared at each other for about five seconds. Then I asked her, "How did that feel?"

"It was awkward, but refreshing."

We hired her to start on the front desk and to provide a bit of assistance to me because the work on my desk was piling up. Elaine was everything she'd portrayed, and much more. She could certainly have grown in the company, but her boyfriend at the time was transferred to northern Alberta, and in times when working remotely was not an option, we sadly had to part ways.

———

"She crumpled it!"

That's what some of my Freshco family members, the shock still evident in their voices, will tell you I did when they handed me their resumé—as if a resumé would contain sufficient information for me to make a decision to hire anyone. I know, I know, that's what the world of corporate constipation teaches: build your resumé. But I prefer to toss said resumés over my shoulder and into the trash can where they belong, then say to my interviewees: "Just tell me who you are."

It's no surprise that nearly 99 percent of the people I interview start off by telling me what school they went to, what degrees they have, what jobs they've held, what they've achieved. It should be equally no surprise that I lean forward with a big smile and say, "That's great. Congratulations. But it's nothing to hang on the line in a rainstorm. So, who are you?"

Many can't answer what should be a very simple question. Have we become so trained by what we think others want to hear that we don't even know who we are? One enema needed to clean out the bullshit. Stat.

Ask me what I'm most proud of, and I'll tell you it's the exceptional group of people with crazy-different personalities and talents who work with me. In my company over the past twenty-five years, I've always respected the fact that every one of us is different and have encouraged all my employees to be themselves. In turn, they show up every day ready to give what they have in their gas tanks—and my company has grown tremendously because of it. I've framed working at Freshco as a lifestyle instead of a "job." It's entrepreneurial in spirit. That means it's high paced, and it can be all encompassing: you have to want to work more for *something* than for yourself. It's not for everybody but, for those who feel at home in Freshco-ville, optimism and energy prevail. When people feel essential, when they can strive to meet their potential, so much can be accomplished without grinding them down or wearing them out. It's extraordinary to have a team of humans from all walks of life embracing and enjoying where they work.

Before joining Freshco, many of my employees either thought they didn't fit in anywhere or felt they did fit in so well, they were ready to start cutting themselves with butter knives. We are, of course, each unique, but the extraordinary people I've hired never before had their individuality embraced. Instead, they felt ostracized—made to feel like outsiders.

But I wouldn't trade them for anything. I love my misfits.

Are you checking to see if you misread that last line? Do I really call my gang "misfits"? I do.

One of my younger team members, Jacob, once looked at me doubtfully over my use of that word, too. Jacob, who's now in a director position, came to us when he was basically in Pampers. He earned increasingly more responsibility and seniority thanks to his hard work, his creativity, and—especially—his different and exciting way of thinking. When we were meeting one day over updating Freshco's brand, I said that I wanted all our misfits to be front and centre in the next marketing campaign.

Jacob frowned. "Don't you think 'misfits' has a negative connotation?"

I smiled. "Yes, Jacob, it did. But so did oatmeal when I was growing up. Now it's a power food that makes you strong and makes you shit."

We laughed. But then he asked again. "Don't you think 'misfit' is negative?"

We talked it over. I realized Jacob didn't share my excitement over the secret power of the misfit because of what being misfit had meant to him growing up. When I was a kid, like everyone else I hung out with my friends at recess, but I remember always being inclusive, trying to bring people together. I wouldn't have been able to articulate it then, but I sensed how different I was on so many levels. And I wanted everyone to feel like they belonged and were accepted for who they were. I came by my radar for misfits naturally.

Jacob, on the other hand, as a white, athletic male, saw sticking out as a negative. The funny thing was, "sticking out" was the very thing that had got Jacob to where he was in the company: his ability to empathize and love more than most; and his refusal just to conform to the mantra of "that's the way it's always been done." He was a guy who'd escaped the expectations of his upbringing and who was not afraid to have the hard conversations—like the one we were having now, with him challenging me, his boss, on the tone and character of our brand. In ways that weren't apparent just by looking at him, in ways that contradicted how easily he'd have fit in early on in life, Jacob was deviant— and that deviance was what I valued in him as an employee and as a person. Maybe he didn't know it, but he was the ultimate misfit.

"Your job is to brand our difference in the industry," I told him. "Get to it." And he did.

"Misfit" has always implied that you're in some way alienated by society and that your "mis-fit" is inherently uncomfortable for you— *and* for those around you. But when *I* say that someone is misfit, I'm saying something positive. When I accept these people into my business and let them be the absolute spectacular human beings they are, it allows them to see that striving to be the world's version of normal is neither fulfilling nor required. You do not have to "fit."

Building a team when you're starting or growing a business is imperative to success, but you can't build just any team. However, if you're going to hire a different type of person, it makes sense to interview differently. So we ask what might be seen as unusual questions—ones that hopefully get me closer to knowing the real person. We might ask an interviewee what kind of construction projects they would take on just for the love of it. We'll throw in a wild card question, like who they'd choose to work alongside if it could be anyone, dead or alive.

Regardless of who I'm interviewing, the process is always based on my gut. I've had more men than I care to count tell me that's a dangerous way to go about doing business. And yet, here I am, boys. I can't apologize for your gut not talking to you the way mine does to me. It's never, ever, let me down.

So give me a resumé and chances are, yes, I'll crumple it up. Anyone can be anything on paper. And frankly, we all know the person who shows up on paper and the person who shows up at work are usually two different people. From the outset, I damn well want to know who you are and what's important to you.

It's a neat thing when people who know they don't fit in out there actually find a home. It's gratifying for me to see my employees light up once they're free to be themselves. You won't find a more loyal, compassionate, eager-to-please bunch of people. Their personalities range from one end of the spectrum to the other: some are filled with life and funnier than shit; others are drier than a merlot in the bowels of the Napa valley. And watching how they respect one another's differences, and make sure others are comfortable in their presence, is staggeringly positive. Because they get it. They know how much that means.

This isn't some radical corporate theory I've tested out. I didn't need any convincing to be sold on the value of hiring misfits. I've never conformed to what the world thinks I should be or how I should behave. I'm living proof that misfits are good for business.

There were lots of ways I stood out growing up. We didn't have it easy at home. We weren't well off, and I sure didn't fit the mould expected of a girl in the 1970s and 1980s. I knew I was different. Heck, I was different in more ways than any of us realized back then. I was gay, but I sure didn't walk around wearing a rainbow T-shirt, because none of us understood it like we do today. Shit, for the longest time, I had no clue why my female friends acted so weird around guys, when they had each other to look at. I kept that to myself, which was confusing, to say the least. But I sensed that to do anything else would be dangerous. Often, when kids don't understand something, their instinct is to make fun of it. Kids can be hateful to those who stand out. For the person on the receiving end of the teasing, that can be devastating.

But I was athletic, a prized skill that took attention away from the things that would've normally given kids cause to bully me. I was even able to stand up for those whose differences really stuck out. I'd say to bullies: "You're gonna stop that now, or this Bear will be all over you like mustard on a baloney sandwich." You won't find a cuddlier, kinder panda than me, but if you hurt somebody who's less privileged, or who's different or marginalized in any way, I will fucking torture your sorry arse until you say "I give!"—and then offer a sincere apology.

I defended misfits because I was damn well aware that, beneath my popularity, I was one of them. It could easily have been me on the other end of the bullying. I often felt I'd gotten away with something.

I'll never forget Nick. We were in high school together in the early 1990s, and he was flamboyant and smart. Nick wore makeup, tight jean shorts with pink shirts, flowing East Indian garments with sandals. He was short. He strutted. Everything about him, to me, screamed, *Suckers! This is what it feels like to be free and express myself!* When I think back to his bravery, I become emotional.

I'm not sure what happened to him after I left Yarmouth, but when we were teenagers, the "boys' club" at school did their damnedest to make him feel unwelcome. What was so desperately sad about the popular people in school was that they could function only in packs. They conformed so completely, it was easy to forget their individual names. They could have easily been labelled A1, A2, A3.

One day, in his usual jovial, carefree manner, Nick was walking down the hallway whistling a tune. Someone from the idiot club threw a handful of pencils and pens on the floor in front of him, then acted like it was an accident. Nick didn't get hurt, but he stopped and, clearly upset, said, "Why do you do this to me?"

I wasn't about to pound the uselessness out of those tits. What was the point? My buddy Trudy, who was also nauseated by their behaviour, helped me get them another way.

It was easy. One of the things about the boy gangs was their predictability. Every Tuesday night, they played basketball and parked their cars next to each other. Just like clockwork. One Tuesday, Trudy and I decided to gift them with organic air fresheners: a supply of fresh, steaming manure from the local dairy farms. I only wish I could have found three roadkill skunks.

We stuffed the manure up their tailpipes and smeared it on their hub caps, with a picture of Nick taped to a tire. They'd see it when they bent their dumb asses down to wash the shit off. The writing on the picture said "We are angels of this human. Keep it up and this will keep happening, because it's not hard to be smarter than any of you." Add a happy face, and we were good to go.

We watched the idiot club for the next couple days to see how they would respond. Aside from asking Nick if he knew who put the shit on their cars, they moved on. The look on Nick's face, knowing someone had messed the "mean boys" up to protect him, was the best.

We all have a little bit of misfit in us. In my world, you can be whoever you want to be. Colour, gender, size, sexuality—heck, you can even like Brussels sprouts for all I care. For me, as a boss, it is always—*always*—do I like you? That's what matters.

Keep in mind, of course, I can read people better than anyone I know, and I'll call you out on your fake bullshit, if that's what I think you're handing out.

So how exactly did Freshco's incredibly cool roster of talented misfits come to be, and why are we so successful? It starts with taking quality over quantity. I don't ever stray from that. We don't hire to fill a space. We hire for talent. I choose to hire minimally. The company seeks out those people I'm instinctively drawn to and, I don't know how I know, but I know they will be loyal.

But instinct and unorthodox hiring practices are only the beginning. We don't just drop people in, to sink or swim. Each new hire is assigned a personal mentor, because we know having a mentor is a game changer in the workplace.

You already know that I lacked a mentor during my own unconventional "apprenticeship," but many people have, at different points, taken me under their wing and taught me what they know. I've also been lucky to experience an accidental taste of the kind of mentorship that brings real vision into the mix—the kind that gives you a new perspective on your goals and your strengths, and where they might lead.

When I say "accidental," I'm not kidding. I might even mean "fate." The Ralph Lauren store on Chicago's Michigan Avenue is my favourite place to shop and eat in the Windy City. Its clothing line and architecture were styles that became "me" many years ago. Four floors of sheer bliss. The bar is no exception, and through those beautiful glass doors reside old-style service and exceptional drinks. I was in town on a business trip. My partner, Sara, was flying to meet me. Her flight was delayed, so I found myself at the bar with a gin martini, comparing notes with the bartender on our East Coast childhoods. He was from Rhode Island and longed, as I did, for a waft of salty ocean air.

A woman on the stool next to me interrupted us.

"Holy shit, eh! What Canadian border did you just cross?"

"Well, you definitely didn't grow up here either," I said to her. "I hear the Queen in your accent."

She laughed. She was born in Baghdad and brought up in London. She shook my hand. "Zaha. My friends call me Curve."

Her stare was piercing, almost intimidating. She was probably twenty years older than me, and wearing a white double-breasted jacket and a pair of green pin-striped pants. The fabric oozed success.

"I do find Canadians charming," she said, eyeing me as she sipped her drink. "What brings you to Chicago, Mandy Rennehan?"

I told her about Freshco, the work I was in town for, and mentioned a few of our Fortune 500 clients. Delighted, she said she was an architect, the one known as "Queen of the Curve." That sure caught my interest. Before I knew it, we weren't just talking shop—we were talking business philosophy, our experiences as women in our industries, all the things that roiled beneath the surfaces of our entrepreneurial minds.

It was massively engrossing. Five hours' worth of engrossing.

A double-Scotch (or more than one), a steak tartare, and a burger later, Curve said, "You blew me away with your story about how you're changing an industry that so badly needs it. But there's one thing I'm puzzled by." She'd Googled me when I went to the washroom and had found, in her words, "very little, if anything, on your greatness."

"Curve," I asked her, "are you a talent agent?" We both laughed.

"Mandy, you're making a difference for sure, but you're keeping your head down. If the world doesn't know about you, your ideas, and this simply funny and charming Canadian who put me in a trance tonight, how will the dial move for you and the industry you care about?" She told me that my combination of credibility and "a huge, real heart" was rare.

She insisted that, to make the change I wanted to make, a change I believed our industry desperately needed, I would absolutely have to become much more of a public face than I was. I'd need to speak; I'd need to consider a TV presence; I'd need to mentor. "You must tie this all together with your philanthropic goals, as this is what will fill your soul while you give out your energy."

Giving out my energy. Did I have a question about this challenge, or was it an answer to why I was so often so damn tired? Something clicked. I realized that, with careful strategizing, I could use my voice and my experience to make real headway in my mission to overhaul my industry. Doing so would bring everything together toward the purpose that drove me, deep down. I could harness my experience *and* my frustration, not to mention my big personality. And doing so would loop some of that spent energy back my way. That was energy I sorely needed.

It was as if Curve had handed me a key to a new path forward, a whole new way of understanding what I'd accomplished, and what I had to offer.

I can't describe the feeling of being in the company of this powerhouse woman. A price tag could never be put on what I gained hearing the trials she'd endured—and overcome—in her decades of experience. A presence like hers, and the wisdom she had to convey, were things I'd so far failed to find but that I'd long craved.

That evening, back in my hotel room, I took out my laptop and Googled Zaha. I was shocked (but at the same time *not* shocked) at what I found. She was a leader in her industry, credited with "liberating" architectural geometry, and the first women ever to receive the Pritzker Architecture Prize. Her work included Michigan's Broad Art Museum, the Maxxi Museum in Rome, and the Guangzhou Opera House. One of her projects underway at the time was the London Aquatics Centre for the 2012 Olympics.

I emailed her later that night, thanking her for one of the most memorable bar dates of my life. "I Googled you," I wrote. "And you're okay."

She wrote back instantly. "Stay humble, Mandy Bear. It's a pinnacle of your real success. I'll be keeping my eye out for what's to come!"

My encounter with Zaha changed my life. We kept in touch until her sudden, premature passing in 2016; she was just sixty-five. In the years since, I've been reminded of her advice and wise counsel often. It has guided and sustained me.

Obviously, I don't want to leave the mentorship of my own people to the randomness of who might sit next to them in a bar. But I know how much that wise counsel, how much access to the reflections of someone with more experience, matters.

At Freshco, we work mentorship into the mix. We do so thoughtfully, with care.

It takes more than a year to mentor and train each staff member. It's a massive investment and undertaking, but it's essential. My bottom line is 10 to 12 percent lower than the industry standard. But I refuse to settle. I'd rather have two of the right people on the job for the right reasons than twenty who are unhappy and are going to leave anyway, which costs me in the long run. My company invests in people: their happiness, their personal and professional development, and their longevity with us.

Confidence happens in stages, and when the world has treated you one way your entire life—when you're a habitual misfit—it might take a hot minute when things suddenly change. When accepted by those around them, people who have had zero self-worth start to grow into powerhouses. But it's one step at a time. First they shift how they walk, how they talk. They need to know who they are, need to understand their worth. Then they need to find where they belong.

At my company, no one fits better than a misfit.

Years ago, my bookkeeper at the time, Laurie, said to me, "Bear, I've got this friend who's in need of a change. Maybe she can work at the front desk?"

That's when Heather walked in. She was shy, quiet, and had less than zero knowledge of the business. She was timid on steroids. But I hired her anyway. There was something about her I liked instantly. And, ooh, I just knew. She would be a game changer.

Heather started part time on the front desk. Timidity aside, she was sharp, a fast learner. But every third word was "sorry."

We had to fix that.

And so I bought a sorry pig: a baby-blue plastic piggy bank that sat proudly on the front desk. Anytime Heather said "sorry" in front of me or anyone else, she had to drop a loonie into the pig. With all those big one-dollar coins, that pig didn't die of malnutrition, that's for sure.

Watching the response from the rest of the crew was hilarious. Heather would say "sorry," and all eyes would immediately turn to her. The crew was kind enough not to laugh out loud. Once or twice a day wouldn't have been half-bad. But, man, Heather said she was sorry a couple times an hour.

It didn't take long for the pig to fill up. That's when I nonchalantly walked over to the counter and emptied out the piggy bank in front of her. Then I rounded up the crew and took everybody out for lunch. I left Heather there. Just walked away with the rest of the staff.

I could tell it took everything she had not to say something. I brought her back a Bear bag full of all kinds of goodies, put them on her desk, looked her in the eyes, and said, "Are you done being subservient to me and everyone else? Because that isn't who you are."

For the first time ever, she looked me square in the face. Then she said, "When you took my fucking money and took everybody out to lunch with it, Mandy, I was so pissed!"

"Perfect. It's about fucking time, because I've been trying to piss you off for over six months."

The change was breathtaking. She immediately owned who she was. I knew all along that Heather was this absolute piranha wanting to escape her quiet, reserved, very back-shelf disposition.

Confidence happens in stages. We learn things every day. Shit, I don't think I really fully matured until this year. Maybe I'm not even there yet. We are, inherently, wisdom-seekers, always wanting more. At times our patience gets the best of us, which is where a lot of anxiety comes from. We are a society of instant gratification. But as much as we think we want immediate results for anything we take on, we need to learn to enjoy the process, ride the wave of each stage, and celebrate each step. You don't suddenly become the most confident person overnight.

Once you get there, though, you discover that confidence comes with a wonderful measure of audaciousness. That's what our trained and mentored team members have. Audaciousness. And for me, there's nothing more beautiful than someone who is not afraid to take a risk.

The great thing about Freshco is that our people know we are a safety net for each other. We don't laugh at those taking risks; we support them. We never consider a risk gone sideways a failure. The only failure, as they say, is in not taking the risk in the first place. By embracing the power of dreaming big and daring wildly, we've created a company full of bold, fun, gutsy employees. That is something to celebrate.

I love that anyone who calls our office will get an employee who is both fun and well informed—comfortable in their own skin. And I'll tell you, the Fortune 500 companies we work with know it and love it. You won't find them hitting redial in the hopes of getting someone else on the line. We're *all* confident, friendly, and pleasant to deal with.

And we all know our shit.

———

"Knowing your shit" means having the hard skills—the technical, analytical, and management skills you need just to do the work, and to do it right. Once mastered, hard skills are amazing—and of course they're necessary to get a job done. Schooling, whether formal or the way I did it—at the school of hard knocks—teaches those hard skills. School is also, of course, where we get the very foundation beneath those skills: the basics of reading, writing, and arithmetic.

It goes without saying that I hire people who have the hard skills, and have them hands down.

Soft skills, in contrast, either come naturally or can be encouraged and developed. They include things like—see Heather's sorry pig earlier—confidence. They include work ethic, communication, problem solving, being a team player. These are the skills that excite me. While hard skills tell me what you can do, soft skills tell me how you will do it—intent, heart, and more. Soft skills, mastered, make a person beautiful.

When you have command of your soft skills, a.k.a. your personality, the mechanical-technical-professional-industrial pieces of the job are more easily grasped. When we feel good, we work better. Our minds are more open to learning the hard shit. We push ourselves. My intent is to have the best of both worlds in my company—hard skills and soft skills—and I do everything I can to encourage growth in both areas.

And, by the way, soft skills shouldn't be labelled as such. They're essential skills, period. With no postsecondary education, no mentors beyond the "get outside and get the stink blown off ya" directive, and no formal training, it's the so-called soft skills like motivation, perseverance, and drive that made me who I am today. It's simple: pride equals performance.

14

GOOD WOMEN BRING WOMEN WITH THEM

Home Depot invited me to give the keynote speech at a national mid-management meeting. The subject? My story, about being a woman in the trades. Of course I said I'd do it. Any opportunity to spread my message about the value women bring to the trades, and what a fantastic career the trades can be for a woman, and I'm there.

When I finished speaking, there was time for questions. A guy put up his hand.

"My daughter is going on four," he said. "And she's the bomb."

I told him everyone thinks their kids are "the bomb." What made him so sure his kid was different?

For starters, he said, she had no interest in dolls. Her thing was blocks. Building things. Construction. You could hear the pride and wonder in his voice. "I grew up in a trades family, and I'm a big promoter of the industry."

Sounded great, but I was still waiting for the question.

"Then my wife said our daughter is not going to trades school. She's going to university."

The room went so silent you could have heard a mosquito fart.

This poor guy was staring at me, red in the face. He was worried, exposed, stuck. What could I possibly say that would help?

"Son," I said, "there is only one piece of advice I can give you. One option only." I paused. "You need to get a goddamn divorce."

There was a time, not so long ago, when a girl would tell her parents she wanted to enter the trades, and her parents would tell her, "No. That's for boys." And wave the idea away like it was ridiculous, just a silly thought.

Wait, what do I mean, not so long ago? It's still happening today.

There's no magic answer to that Home Depot guy's dilemma. You fall in love, you have kids. Kids grow up. We say we're teaching them independence and then, instead of letting them follow their aspirations, we funnel them into our own dreams for their futures. What the kids want, what makes their hearts sing, falls to the wayside.

(For the record, when I gave that speech, I was impressed by the diversity of these folks. My hat goes off to Home Depot: I know they're doing things right, both in their hiring practices and in their training.)

The barriers to getting women into the trades start even before they're born. But they don't end there.

Even worse than being steered away from the trades by their parents, some girls, picking up on the attitudes around them, convince *themselves*. They don't even entertain the trades as an option.

I was sitting with a friend at the North York Civic Centre in Toronto's Mel Lastman Square after her TED talk. Head of a big PR firm, she was my publicist. Despite her very public profession, she happened to be deathly afraid of public speaking. So the day of her talk, which was called "Showing Up," a bunch of us did just that: we showed up to offer moral support.

Afterward, we all went across the street for a celebratory dinner. She'd rented the whole upstairs of a local restaurant. I knew some of her staff, and ended up sitting next to her niece. I asked what she was studying.

"I might want to do PR," she said. "Like my aunt."

"Oh, your aunt is the queen of PR," I replied.

"I know, but mom said no. She told me I have to go to university to become a doctor or lawyer."

"Maybe you'll go to college," I said, "and study a trade."

Instantly, her body language changed. Her eyes changed. "Oh, no," she said. "I could never do that. The trades are dirty."

I liked this young lady, so it was important for me to help her understand the truth. "I'm blue collar."

The look on her face was priceless. "No, you're not."

"Sweetie, I'm blue collar," I repeated.

"Mandy, you're not what I think of when I think blue collar and the trades."

She wasn't trying to be rude. It never dawned on her. This was her truth. This was how she'd been raised: to believe that blue collar people are second class, and they're dirty, and that a career in the trades was not even something for her to remotely consider. And because I was in beautiful, expensive clothing—that's right, I'm a hot-tie in French and Italian designers—I was automatically white collar, even to an eighteen-year-old. Wow.

Dumb-ass expectations for girls sure as hell existed when I was growing up. Thank Christ, somehow, they bounced right off me. It never dawned on me that I'd be treated a certain way because I was a girl—or that there were expectations that I'd get myself a boyfriend, get married, have a heaping helping of kids. My own mother didn't know what made her happy: she looked after us kids; she cooked; she cleaned. She had children she loved dearly, but she never got the chance to understand herself. Any aspirations that may have snuck into her life were quickly suppressed. Somehow, I escaped that fate—maybe because I was keenly aware of what my mother hadn't even had the chance to imagine for herself. If anyone had been stupid enough to suggest a future in the kitchen for me, they wouldn't be around today to tell the story—or at the very least, they'd be walking funny.

When I started in the trades in the mid-1990s, I was always the only female on a job site. It wasn't much different from what I'd been used to. I grew up with brothers. All the kids on my street were boys. All the people I played sports with were boys. I'd worked with boys on the farms. Imbalanced as it was, that environment was comfortable for me. But not entirely. I still felt the pressure of being the only female on the site: I didn't want to embarrass myself or let the owner down, especially after he'd given this girl the chance to come onsite and learn. There's a lot of earthquaking going on in your mind in that situation. I'd just tell myself, day after day, that I'd better make damn sure I was useful.

As of 2012, nearly twenty years later, women still held fewer than 6 percent of all construction jobs. Even now, another decade on, if you take the trades as a whole, women's representation drops right down to 4 percent. One, two, three, four. You don't even need a whole hand to count it out. I've been at this for coming up on three decades, and the industry *still* functions at 96 percent male. Hear me when I say that nothing progressive will ever come of that.

Just like when I, a woman, turned up on those all-male job sites in the mid-nineties, I remain an anomaly. Only now, I run a multi-million-dollar empire. And in this stubbornly male-dominated industry of construction and maintenance, 60 percent—yes, that's six-zero—of my workforce is female. Just as importantly, they damn well make what they're worth. They do from day one. They go through the exact same channels as the men to learn their skills, and they deserve no less.

The women we hire don't have to be built like me to be dynamite on the job site, by the way. Freshco was the first company in Canada to use the Fortis exoskeleton to reduce fatigue and injury. Built by Lockheed Martin, this marvellous piece of technology allows the wearer to hold heavy tools for a long period. And that sultry piece of equipment on a petite female on a construction job is an awesome sight. We bought this technology right out of the gate, when it was still working its way toward its optimal possibilities, and the system we use does have its limits. It's great for demolition work, but not always adaptable to other tasks. We closely monitor developments in this area and will absolutely keep pace with exoskeleton technology as it develops, because the burn rate of someone's muscles needs to be at the forefront of how the trades industry goes forward.

Meanwhile, moving that needle to get more women involved is not a pet project for me. It's part of my makeup. It's part of my DNA. Suppose, just suppose, that the trades went from 4 percent female to *40 percent* female. You can bet your arse that would change everything. Everything. Because one woman in the trades is a goddamn army.

A few years ago, the boys and I were in Vegas having a work weekend on the golf course. Or something like that. Before I'd hit forty, I had somehow underestimated the benefits of the spa. Probably because I was so busy. Or maybe the thought of a naked Bear, perspiring heavily and surrounded by sweaty strangers, didn't make the cut. But now I was in my forties, and when you're in Vegas . . .

Off I shuffled to the steamroom to rest my weary muscles. Wrapped snug in a luxurious towel, I leaned my head back, started to relax, and was snapped out of my reverie by the woman across from me.

"It's you! The lady from the cooking network! It's you!"

I had to tell my steamy little friend across the way that she was mistaken. "Not Lynn Crawford. But I am the Blue Collar CEO," I said, figuring she'd have no idea what that meant.

There were three other women in the sauna, and they all jumped to attention at once.

"Oh, my goodness," one of them said. "You're that woman who's in construction."

I smiled. You got me.

The woman could hardly believe the coincidence. "We're all here in Vegas," she said, "because we needed a break after each going through our own nightmares with people who call themselves contractors. We're from California, but we had to get away, it was that exhausting."

Now I love a good "shit on the shitty contractor" story, but at that moment, I just wanted the steam to make love to my pores and get some of this golfing soreness out of me. But these women insisted on telling me their stories. And good ones they were. "Good" in the sense of off-the-charts awful.

"My husband and I got divorced because of renovations," one of them said.

I opened one eye. Shocking, but . . . not.

I'd heard it all—or I thought I had. Folks share their construction horror stories with me regularly. They aren't few and far between.

One time a friend called me from Muskoka, in Ontario's cottage country, where her daughter was to be married on a landing overlooking the water. The contractors they'd hired had built not even half the deck, then vanished. They just walked away with their deposit. They also stole a buggy from the property.

Similar, yet worse: a woman I had been dealing with at a banking institution told me the story of her great-aunt, an elderly lady in Niagara. The contractors had come to her home and gutted it, then left it that way.

I had to ask. "How much did your aunt give them?"

"Fifty thousand dollars," she said.

"They told her the total cost of the renovations would be eighty-six thousand. She has the rest in her savings still, but they just up and left her without finishing the job!"

No one deserves to be treated like that, but a senior? She was seventy-three years old. This house was her whole retirement. She was devastated, she was heartbroken, she was angry. She had a chronic health issue, which the stress was making worse.

I wanted to help this woman. It helped that from the moment I met her, I adored her. I also talked her down off the bridge. I told her, "Everything happens for a reason. Now that you have me here, it will get done better." It wasn't normally a job I'd take on, but it became an angel project for me. A friend of mine had an apartment he was waiting to let to a student, and he happened to owe me a favour. I said to him, I need a month. I need this woman and her cat Muffin to be happy and not have to deal with the absolute tragedy of living in a home that's being renovated.

Thankfully I have a shop and could do the work for her at cost. So instead of charging her fifty thousand dollars for the cabinetry, I was able to do it for twenty thousand. And we were able to come in and do everything within the month. I basically took the money she had left for the work and used it on supplies and some of my labour. I was probably out thirty thousand dollars in the end. I didn't care about the money, except that somehow, someone else's unprincipled behaviour had cost *me*. I hoped I never laid eyes on those contractors—ever. She said dealing with us, compared to the company that had defrauded her, was like the difference between night and day.

Awful, right? But the stories I heard from the women in the Las Vegas steamroom were just as unreal. One of them had signed a contract for a renovation with a three-month timeline. Thrilled about the quick schedule, she'd paid a 70 percent deposit. More than a year later, the company was still doing the work and had barely made headway. Before this woman had left for Las Vegas, the main washroom was supposed to be plumbed—but it hadn't yet happened, and nobody had heard from anybody. She said, "We don't have $350,000 to give to somebody else to take over. It's gone."

Another woman was restoring a home she and her husband had bought in Seattle. They'd hired a so-called restoration company that came in, ripped out original features, and replaced them with cheap replicas. She questioned the contractor, who said that if they didn't use replicas the work would have taken years. She replied, "Yes, that's exactly what we discussed." He defended the "work" he'd done, saying, "I've made a template. Nobody will ever know the difference."

But she and her family would know. And this was not what they'd paid for. They called a lawyer who helped them bring a cease-and-desist order against the company. The contractor was instructed to put everything back the way it was. But of course only half of it came back, and all of it half-ruined.

And in that confined space, with sweat running down my cheeks (all of them), I knew I had to find a way to push harder against this insipid bullshit.

When I returned from Vegas, I decided to test out a theory. I asked my friend whose great-aunt had been left high and dry, "Was nobody helping her?"

Her answer hit the nail on the head.

"Mandy," she said, "If there were women in the trades, this would never have happened."

So I put it out there, on Twitter, Facebook, Instagram. One question: "How would you feel if a female contractor showed up at your house?"

It went viral. It was shared thousands and thousands of times.

A whole population of women were like, holy shit, please; yes, please. They loved that possibility. Even in the medical system, there are people who are going to feel more comfortable with a female. Why should your family doctor, your dentist, or your massage therapist be any different from your general contractor? An inordinate amount of men thought a woman would make a better general contractor than a man would. Ninety percent of the response to the post was positive. Maybe 7 percent of men took the post to heart; their insecurity made them behave like trolls. Another 3 percent were just trolls.

Women do things differently. We're more organized, we'll break everything down for you from an analytical perspective. We're determined to get the job done right the first time around, as opposed to half-assing it and figuring we can fix it later on if need be. (What the hell is that all about? Just do shit right the first time.)

There are good male contractors out there—of course there are. Without a doubt. But somewhere in their organizations—in most of them—those men are backed by women, and they will be the first to admit that to you. I'm not suggesting we replace men with women, just that we bring both to the table, as I've done in my company. You cannot have any industry controlled entirely by men and expect excellence. Women coming in have made those men better, just as the men are able to nudge women along in the ways *they're* better. Men are beautiful problem solvers onsite. They're tactical. They're polymaths. Even, often, artists. They think on their feet. But too often, they don't know how to multitask. They're not planners. They make promises all over the place that they can't keep, they burn out, and they leave people in the lurch. And then you just get the crooks. The crooks communicate better than anybody: that's how they sell you on their shit. There are a lot of skilled and principled guys out there, but it would appear there aren't enough of the good ones to go around—and the bad ones ruin it for the rest.

Some of the men get it. I've had quite a few men on my team approach me and ask, "Hey, can you send us more women?"

"Why?" I ask them, with a knowing smile. I want them to have to say it.

"Because they listen," they'll say.

"They're awesome." "They're loyal." "They're fastidious."

"I trust them more driving a truck after two weeks than the guys I've had for two years."

Damn, I love hearing men talk like that. It's almost hot. But—not. Women have a different set of skills. Some women may take an extra fifteen minutes to map out a job, and that means I charge an extra fifteen minutes upfront.

But the work won't have to be done twice. Even the men know this.

One woman in the trades is a goddamn army.

Let that sink in.

Turning these stats around is no mission for the faint of heart. When you have one hundred guys to one woman on a worksite, that's a problem. But when those guys think it's even remotely okay to treat the woman differently, look out. That's another thing altogether.

Fact: most men on a job site will treat a female colleague well. But you'll get 10 to 15 percent so neck deep in their backward, misogynist, bullshit thinking that they don't even understand why a woman is there, never mind realize she has more talent than they do. Add to that, men have always had the freedom to speak however they want: there have been no women on the job site and, thus, no accountability.

Well, bud, the times they are a-changin'. But they sure as hell aren't changin' overnight. It's more like molasses speed—and molasses, if you're not careful, can gum things up.

Companies come to me often, wanting to see more diversity in their teams.

"We want more women," they tell me. That includes female airplane mechanics, truck drivers, plumbers—the gamut.

"Great," I say. "But do you have a structure or human resource strategy in place that supports what you're asking for?"

The phone usually goes silent.

Women in general, but especially in the trades industry, come with a separate set of instructions. We're like fine washables, only more durable than denim.

You can't just throw women out on job sites with men, in an environment where there have been few or no women before, and hope for the best. Women need to have their own washrooms. Women need to be supported by human resources and protected from sexual harassment. That means zero tolerance. They need to be able to pick out workwear that fits their frame and that doesn't put them at risk of injury. Women are genetically made to have babies: you need to have a plan in place that supports them through pregnancy. All these things, that have never (or almost never) been looked at, come into play.

Being a female in the trades is difficult enough, but a female entrepreneur? It's ugly. I'm humbled to have had awards and doctorate degrees bestowed on me. I love the example this sets for everyone, and that it gives hope to women, telling them it's not just the male CEOs who can take on the world. It was finally time for the companies that sponsor these awards to recognize talent for talent.

The response to my winning these awards is very telling. The males in CEO positions who are great at what they do, and who understand the need for diversity in the corporate world—in all worlds, goddammit—and for recognizing talent regardless of gender, are the first ones to grab my hand and congratulate me.

Then there are the other CEOs—those whose title stands for Chief Ego Officer—who don't know what to do except be angry, because they don't understand how a woman could win a top business or academic prize. These idiot sticks think "I date women" makes them experts in diversity. It's pathetic.

The problem isn't just in the boardroom. Consumer expectations are unrealistic as it is, but when clients value what a female entrepreneur does less than what a male does—and assume they can pay less—we have a disconnect that sends me over the cliff.

I was in St. John's, Newfoundland, one of my favourite places, having a chat with a local entrepreneur. She told me one of the biggest obstacles in business, for her, was that people wanted everything done for nothing.

"What do we do?" she asked.

"You have to educate people on the value of what you do. Ask them why they are insisting you go out of business."

She looked puzzled.

"They make requests of you that are ridiculous, and you are caving in, out of fear of losing a client."

She nodded. I was right.

I shook my head to tell her that approach was all wrong. "Let them know they walked into your shop, you're credible in your field, and they're asking you to go out of business by insisting on that price for that product. Then look at their faces."

Her smile was nervous, but enlightened.

"Set your price and stick with it. Period. They won't value you unless you value yourself."

It's part of my mission to help young women understand they don't have to do their work for nothing. In my hometown of Yarmouth, Julie Mood is a young female entrepreneur going through the same issues, but she's learning fast.

Julie, a.k.a. Mini, has both personality and heart, and she's not only learning the value of what she does, she's learning to share that knowledge with her clients. She owns Julie Mood Interiors, and she can build anything from coffee tables to kitchens. Wood and metal love her. So do her clients. They respect her way of doing business, and they love her work. Win–win. Mini and I have partnered on transforming some local buildings I purchased into high-end apartments and one-of-a-kind business opportunities. We talk every day, and I love that she isn't afraid to share the good, bad, and ugly with me—and that I'm able to kick her arse if I have to.

I've told Mini many times, "I can see that you leave a piece of your heart in every build, so don't be shy about telling your clients that." And she listens. She tells them.

It's not only our young female entrepreneurs who are questioned. It's me, too. I'm at the top of my game, working daily with Fortune 500 companies, and I still get challenged on price points.

"You're too high," I was recently told.

Here we go again, I thought. "Compared to what?"

"Compared to the other vendors who responded to the RFP," they said, surely thinking I'd cave.

"Yes, I'm sure I am a bit higher. If you're comparing only numbers, I'll probably lose every time. But what intrinsic value are they bringing to the table? Because, you know, I bring a shitload of it."

I'd rather go out of business than not stick to my fucking value. Value is more than a number. Part of value is experience. Part is sticking to timelines. Part is going above and beyond. Part is the highly qualified team I bring to the table. Another part is my commitment to follow up. I'm always fully transparent with my clients. They won't be surprised by hidden costs. Should anything go wrong, they won't be left to their own devices. That matters.

It's part of my mission to educate people on what it's like to be "her": that extraordinarily talented female entrepreneur, business owner, tradesperson. All this somehow reminds me of women in politics, another rare species. Those female political leaders who put themselves out there; make the best decisions for the right reasons; are transparent, with zero political spin on their decisions; make little money; and get their heads kicked in by ignorant arseholes day and night. It's no damn wonder more women don't step up into politics, either.

Shit, people. We are our own worst enemies on more than one front.

If being a woman in the trades (or the boardroom) is difficult, add on moving through the world as a gay person and see where that lands. The level of ignorance that I sometimes encounter on this front is off the charts.

I was sitting in an airport in Dallas waiting for the weather to change in Toronto so I could fly home. The bar was full, and the guy next to me, looking pitifully despondent said, "You know, it sucks to be me some days."

I felt like I was in a rerun of *The Golden Girls*, wearing Dorothy's scowl after Rose has made a dumb comment. This guy took sulking to another level.

One never knows what another person is going through, so I thought: Bear, be nice. Maybe this man has lost a loved one, or has just received terrible news, and needs someone to talk to. I took a double gulp of my beer and readied myself. "What troubles you, my friend?"

His wife and daughter were upset with him. Why? "Because I stayed an extra two days in Dallas to watch some football with my friends." I could see how that might ruffle some feathers. But there was more. "I missed my grandmother's ninetieth birthday party."

Wait. What?

There was a small part of me that wanted to slam his head off the bar. But I politely said, "Yup, son, it must be rough." Then I laughed, because I couldn't help myself.

"Well, I'm sure you don't have these issues with your husband."

Dear God, hand me the butter knife so I can start my slow death from my ankles. I turned to him and said, "My husband is a woman. And, no, I can't say I've ever had those issues."

He looked shocked. I took a generous gulp of my drink and reached for my bags, so I could get the hell out of there. I wasn't fast enough.

"Can I ask you something?"

I was silent, thinking if this son of an idiot-stick asks me if I know so-and-so from Canada, like there are only three families there, I really will bounce his head off the bar.

"Was it hard for you when you decided to pick being gay?"

I threw my head back because I needed to catch my breath. His sheer stupidity had sucked all the air out of the room.

I pulled my chair close, stared him straight in the eyes, and said, "You picked missing your grandmother's party. I did not pick gay. It picked me. And because you are so unbelievably stunned and ignorant, you can pick up the fucking tab for this Canadian girl who didn't choose to be gay, but is. Because, well, it's the fair thing to do!"

"I didn't mean to offend you," he said.

"You didn't," I replied.

You just re-enforced why I always need a direct flight, and why I should always put a bag on the seat next to me in an airport bar.

If we are going to call out the women-in-the-trades bullshit for what it is, we have to make sure we recognize, fully, what we are dealing with. That means understanding the difference between being mistreated or bullied in a toxic workplace, and dealing with the pure and simple ignorance you encounter in an unprogressive workplace. The enlightenment will serve us well.

Mini called to chat one day. She was worried about her friend Agnes, who had recently become a Red Seal welder. Agnes had stopped by the shop to tell Mini that she was giving it up: leaving welding and heading to massage therapy school. She'd dealt with some hurtful stuff at work, and she'd had enough.

Mini, being Mini, tried to talk her out of it. "I'll hire you," she told her friend. She believed in her that much. But Agnes wasn't having it.

I happened to be in Yarmouth, and Mini asked if I'd have a Mandy chat with Agnes. Of course I would. We got together for a heart-to-heart. My reaction, and any advice I might have, I warned her, would be blunt but honest.

Agnes felt she'd been bullied in her workplace. She told me her story. I listened and, by what she said, formed a picture in my mind: not of a bullied young woman but of one with expectations that were far from being met. They were fine expectations, great ones, even— exactly what you want from a well-run business. She wanted to work in a company that had strong leadership. She wanted her innovative ideas and her suggestions for improving efficiency to be heard.

Not everybody runs companies like mine. I wish they did. But Agnes had started working for an established company in a fishing community that had, as far as the people in charge could tell, succeeded perfectly well being run as it always was, thank you very much. They didn't know what to do with her, because they weren't yet where she was. We can't expect an entire workplace culture— messed up as it is—to change overnight. And we can't save them from themselves. I wasn't making excuses for them. It's reality.

I told her to take a step back and look at the big picture—the effect her presence might have on a workplace that hadn't changed in decades. Not just as a woman, but also as someone who'd gone away and come back. There had to be a bit of jealousy on the part of the old boys where she was concerned. Possibly confusion. Maybe even fear.

I told her the self-professed rural cowboys she was working with had probably never been on a plane, while she had lived in major cities where she'd worked for larger, more formally structured companies. She was experienced and educated in her field. Coming back to small-town Nova Scotia would throw anyone off.

"Are you going to let somebody who has never worked with a woman in the trades, never been taught how to respect a woman in the trades because the company has never gotten that far yet, because they have zero competition—are you going to let them take away your chosen career? You're going to let them force you to put away those Red Seal skills that you worked your ass off for?"

I let her think on that, then I continued.

"And, because one of them is smoking in the truck and it's against the rule book you were given, you are giving up on who you are? This is not their fault. It's yours. They aren't the issue. You're the issue."

Consumers want Agneses. They're starved for talent like hers, and female talent more so. She had an expectation of what a work environment should be, but it was her job to navigate around the bullshit. Lots of companies out there have zero tolerance for discrimination or bullying, but they're still dinosaurs in terms of the way they operate—they're so unprogressive that if you're someone coming in with new ideas they don't see the merit in, you either can't be there or you need to suck it up and stop complaining. I told her she had the freedom to get out and go to massage therapy school or whatever path she chose, but I warned her, "Do *not* confuse bullying with ignorance. They're different."

"You're right, Mandy," she told me, through tears. "They didn't want to see my point of view. They didn't even try to understand what I was saying."

"That's right, sweetie. Because they were so completely intimidated by you, your skills, your life experience. It's unfortunate. But welcome to being popular and powerful. It's fucking lonely at times. But I'll tell you what. Wow, is it fiery! And it pays the damn bills. And it makes you go home at night and think about how you can make sure that what happened to you, doesn't happen to other women."

I didn't want to be any harder on her than I already had been, but she needed to hear what I was saying. "You've got to know that why you're giving up is a very short-sighted way of looking at things. You just want to give up because somebody didn't want to listen to you. Well, poor fucking you. Let me tell you about the women out there who have been throttled by beatings, or who've devoted their lives to paving the way for you to have an opinion and options. Including me, who drove 1oo kilometres an hour on a 70-kilometre stretch so I could give you fifteen minutes of my time to tell you to take your head out of your ass. And to tell you that I can't do this alone. I need people like you to do this with me. So let's get up, brush off the poor me, and get moving."

She smiled. Now that I'd given her the tough talk, it was time to start building her back up.

"You, my dear, have talent. You're young, beautiful, and I can see you've got a fire in you. If you showed up on my doorstep with an iPad ready to do a floor plan for a renovation, I would have to tell you to hang on for a second because I would be that damn excited that *you*, a female, showed up at *my door*. Remember how excited you were to start your course and how accomplished you felt when you finished? You were fucking made for this. Now give us a big hug, and I gotta go."

Later, Mini called and told me, "Mandy, she's a mess, but a good mess."

"Yup," I said. "We have to stop teaching kids to just give up. Dammit, the 'hard' is the GD orgasm in the sex scene. Getting through the 'hard' parts of life is euphoric."

Mini hired Agnes, the Red Seal welder, and they're a force to be reckoned with. It's a beautiful thing.

Mini is exactly the kind of person we need to build up our army of female entrepreneurs. She hosts "Shop the HERd" events in her showroom twice a year and invites female entrepreneurs in to showcase and sell their products. It's astounding to watch as the women in this pop-up collective support one another. One young woman who has a charcuterie board business has Mini build the boards, and they cross-market. When Mini builds kitchens for her clients, she leaves a board with them. Another woman, who works with flowers, uses Mini's shop and products as a backdrop, and Mini makes sure she has fresh flowers in the shop to showcase. She leaves flowers in her kitchens, too. There's no shortage of ways to market when they pull together, and their clients are inspired by these female-strong events.

Like Mini, I do whatever I can, whenever I can, to help women in the trades. Men are not the only problem with women in the trades. Women are an issue, too. Men, stuck in the systemic pattern of exclusion, are grappling with their insecurity and confusion right now: they don't know what the hell to do with women in the trades. But there are also successful women who, while they have no problem taking men with them, leave other women behind. Nothing is more wasteful than a woman at the top who has not brought other women with her. That grinds my gears. It needs to change. Stop that shit. Just stop it.

Aside from my hiring practices, working with Conestoga College in Kitchener, Ontario, is one of my favourite ways of bringing other women along. I bring my team to the college regularly to mentor their Women in Skilled Trades (WIST) students, and I participate in their very cool Jill of All Trades and other events. I love WIST, a tuition-free program funded by the provincial government to support low-income women who are unemployed or underemployed as they prepare for careers as general carpenters within the construction sector. WIST students learn the basic skills required to secure a position as an apprentice. The thirty-four-week program includes twenty-six weeks of in-class practical theory and hands-on experience, and a paid eight-week work placement. Wahoo! Roll out the women! At Christmas, I give each student five hundred dollars to help subsidize their living expenses. We don't want anyone's circumstances to stop them from pursuing their dreams.

I also speak to women any chance I get. I want them to understand what a beautiful career path the trades can offer: it's lucrative (I'm proof of that) and fulfilling. Most importantly, they can be part of it. We need to start sharing that message and stop the ridiculous conversations about how women don't fit.

Good men support women. Good women bring women with them.

15

LAUGHTER'S GOOD FOR THE SOUL— AND FOR BUSINESS

Bear! You've been in the washroom for over half an hour. What in the love of God are you doing in there? I'm getting worried!"

I'd been in a trance, and Annie had just snapped me out of it.

We were in Vienna, where we'd gone for Christmas so we wouldn't have to decide between spending the holidays with her family or mine. Budapest and Prague were also on our itinerary. We would meet our families in the new year.

What you need to know is that Eastern European architecture gives me chills. I *love* it. Our Vienna hotel room was something out of a 1920s design magazine. Including the washroom.

I'd gone in there to get ready to go out for dinner with Annie.

Hang on for a sec. Before we go further into our Viennese adventure, I need to tell you a little something about Annie, my partner and the love of my life. I'm taking a risk, here. Me veering off like this in the midst of an anecdote is just the thing that's liable to have Annie accusing me of falling back into my squirrel complex.

A "squirrel complex" is what I suffered from before Annie came into my life. My PR queen, Taunia, would say to me, "Bear, you're a great speaker, but . . ."

The "but" was that, while giving a speech, I'd get onto a subject and then get onto something else, and just keep going: I'd forget to circle back. Taunia said there was only one woman to call in a situation such as mine: Lauren Ferraro, *the* person Canadian celebrities and senior executives turn to when they want to up their public-speaking game. That's how I found myself, one afternoon in March 2017, face to face with Lauren at table 27 of the signature restaurant of the Shangri-La Hotel in downtown Toronto—my go-to meeting spot. I was skeptical. As was she. Lauren told Taunia she would need eight sessions with me to polish my technique, to which I had declared, "I'm not having eight sessions with anybody." There'd been a good deal of back-and-forth before we managed to set up this one initial meeting.

As it happens, I was right. It took only twenty minutes for Lauren to fix my squirrel complex. She told me to listen to the question I'd been asked and focus on taking my reply right to the end, before I let my thoughts lead me somewhere else. Either I was a super-quick study, or she was a way better teacher than she was willing to admit. Either way, that was it; that was all I needed.

But it wasn't all I needed, or wanted, of Lauren. We stayed at that table for hours, talking. Finally, she looked me in the eye and said, "I can't be attracted to a client."

I coolly replied, "We're adults."

End of story. Or, more like the beginning of the story of the love of my life.

And, of course, everyone knows, no matter how old you are, you bring the love of your life home to meet your parents. When Pup first set eyes on Lauren and her head of blazing red hair, he said, "I never knew how pretty Anne of Green Gables was in person." Half an hour later he was talking about how much he loved the movie *Annie Get Your Gun.*

Lauren's nickname was sealed.

Okay. Now I'm circling back to Christmas in Vienna. See? Still squirrel-complex-cured! Remember what was going on? Poor Annie—who, by the way, still loves to remind me that I never paid her invoice for that session—had begun to think I might never emerge from the hotel washroom. The truth is, I'd gotten distracted by the tile work in there: the grout lines, the corner marks, the quality of the levelling. It was obvious to me that this tile work wasn't just a job for the person who had taken it on. It was the most exceptional I'd seen in my life. It was sheer perfection. That mysterious someone in the European tile and stone industry had put their heart and soul into this work. And I was in awe.

Had Annie walked through the door, she'd have seen me on all fours, running my hands along the tiles like they were some kind of sexual objects. Time had passed by in the blink of an eye.

"I'm taking pictures, Annie!" I called out to her. "The tile work in here is so goddamn amazing I can't even stand myself."

Eventually, she was able to pry me away, and we went out for the evening. We still laugh about me and that stunning tile work. I'm a germaphobe, so it would take something mighty special to get me on a washroom floor.

It's this kind of thrill—this joy and pride in the work—that I aim to foster in my team members. I want them to love their jobs as much as I love mine, to care enough about perfecting their own skills to be able to suddenly find themselves on all fours, inspecting the gorgeous tile work on the floor of a hotel washroom—and to see, in the midst of that passionate impulse, how hilarious that is. I want them to give it their all, but to enjoy themselves, even laugh at themselves, in the process.

Hello there. Thanks for calling Freshco, NOT the grocery store! It seems someone's slacking on the phone lines but not to worry. You've reached Canada's most amazing, trendy, and fun maintenance and retail construction specialist ... If you know the extension of the superstar you'd like to reach, feel free to cut me off by dialling their extension now ... If you're still not sure, not to worry. Stay on the line and our gatekeeper will be with you shortly.

Won't you, Trev?

[Trev's voice:] I guess.

Want to kill your business? Put employee well-being on the back burner. Holy shit, it's deadly. I committed from the very beginning to making fun a priority, part of our culture. Laughter excites the soul and induces a rush of serotonin, which results in a burst of positive energy. That energy is freeing and encourages a different way of looking at work and life. Who wants to be tied down to the old mundane way of thinking? Not us! So in our otherwise conservative industry—from our phone message, to our setup, to staff activities—Freshco is known as the "fun company."

But we can't just say it. We have to deliver. And we do.

The first thing you see when you make your way into Freshco's headquarters in Oakville, Ontario, is a wall display of hand-drawn caricatures of our team members, a nickname beneath each drawing. They may be hand-drawn cartoons, but they magically capture the essence of each person. Within a few days of being hired, you'll be on the wall.

The first drawing is of the person you'll have to get through to see me. You'd have to be as stealthy as Catwoman on the prowl for a café latte to get by The Gatekeeper. The Gatekeeper is my twin, Trev, our greeter who makes the Guardians of the Galaxy look like amateurs. He'll treat you with the utmost respect, and he knows where every team member is, and to whom to direct any question that comes his way. But you won't get past him without one hell of a good reason.

Like Trev, a.k.a. The Gatekeeper, everyone on my team has a nickname. And I only have to know you as long as a blink to know what your new name will be. Sometimes there's a full-blown story that goes with the name. Most times it's a word you say or something you do, and *bam!*—that's your nickname. And the names stick. The nickname goes on the business card of each team member and on everyone's work gear, including the comfy hoodies we provide. Good luck asking for someone by their given name in the office or on the job site. No one will know who the hell you're talking about.

Heather, my chief operating officer (she of the sorry pig in Chapter 13), earned her nickname on a business trip to Vancouver.

Shortly after Heather was hired to help out at the front desk, long before her COO days, I'd switched her from part time to full time. She was the complete opposite of me. I was hyper; she was calm. I was quick on the draw; she took her time. I was loud; she was quiet. I love Scotch; she loved vodka. She was fourteen years my senior, she'd lived through adversity, and I saw what she could be. I pushed her out of her comfort zone. She'd dislike me for it one day, then hug me the next.

I had to fly out to Vancouver because we were working with lululemon, which at the time was in serious expansion mode. I brought

Heather along because I knew by then that she would soon be my secret weapon.

We arrived safely and headed to our rooms. We'd never travelled together, so she'd have to get to know my idiosyncrasies. I told her I was fastidious about my shirts but that I didn't iron very well. She told me no problem. We left it at that.

I knocked on her door at quarter to five in the morning, shirts in hand. A pause, and the door flew open. She stood before me, in Mickey Mouse pajamas, in a full-blown panic. I asked if she was okay.

"Yup, I'll be fine. When do you want these done?"

The meeting was at 8:30, so, if the shirts were done by 7:30, that would be great. I was testing her. In fact, I'm always testing people. To make this fat story thin, my shirts were perfect, we landed another nice deal, and that evening we went for dinner. I asked Heather about her panic that morning. I figured it was me showing up so early that had caused it.

"You looked scared shitless," I said.

But she surprised me. It wasn't me turning up at 5 a.m. that had thrown her off. It turns out that, on her way to answer the door, she'd seen her shadow out of the corner of her eye. For a second, she thought there was someone in the room. She was startled. Beyond startled, by the state of her when she opened that door: completely freaked out.

That story got Heather two things from me. First, a full-blown belly laugh. And second, her nickname.

I dub thee "Shadow."

In the long run, the name turned out to be more appropriate than I could have anticipated. Shadow became the very epitome of the "shadow" behind every successful or influential person who's ever lived. She was my shadow—and that's exactly what she wanted to be.

She didn't want to be in the spotlight. She wanted to make me and the company better. A person with that kind of innate courtesy, that level of comfort within themselves, is rare and remarkable, because people are usually competing instead of collaborating. But Shadow and I, working together, made a formidable force.

There's been much said about work–life balance throughout the years, but I disagree with the philosophy of separating our work from the rest of life. This doesn't mean I believe in people working themselves ragged. Part of Freshco's culture is about living one life, not two, which means our team members don't have to pretend to be someone else when they come to work. The real them showing up is what matters. Over time, this approach benefits them as well as the company.

These "real" people showing up at Freshco every day work hard—they work their asses off. The environment in which they do that work matters. We equip our space with standing desks, because, frankly, sitting on your ass is a waste of a good life, and I don't want to be responsible for that. We have ping-pong tables because we all need a break, and they're great for thinking on your feet. There's beer in the fridge for special occasions, keeping in mind that "special" is relative.

Which brings me to the flip side: While my team and I work hard, we also play hard. We have tried every pastime known to humanity, from trampoline bouncing to laser tag, and we don't care if we're good at the activities we take on because it's being together, laughing, and enjoying our time that matters most—team building at its best. We're always up for something new, and our monthly meet-ups for axe-throwing competitions are proof of that. (So far, no one has been hurt.)

Sometimes, I admit, our "fun" is a bit mischievous. Freshco had two new employees starting at the same time. Their first day coincided with the arrival of our new recycling bins. Two of my senior people had the bins set up strategically so they could, at just the right moment, jump out of the bins and scare the living shit out of our new arrivals.

"You're welcome," we said, once they'd calmed down enough to laugh at the prank—and to wonder what the hell they'd got themselves into.

The advancements in technology over the years have made working in the trades a different game altogether. Gone are the days where it's the "same old–same old," when we would go to work feeling like there was nothing new on the horizon. Yawn.

Because our team is ready mentally, and trained physically, we have become leaders in our field in a way that some find difficult to grasp. Our team was the first to bring 3D-modelling cameras to our customers. We masterfully operate computer numerical control (CNC) machines daily, carving out the sexiest lines ever seen. A CNC machine is a robotic carver that can be programmed to cut anything out of metal, glass, wood—name your substance. It can carve woodwork, it can carve signs, it can carve pictures.

We use this sort of high-end equipment to deliver unparalleled quality—but we also make sure we don't pass up an opportunity to put smiles on people's faces, whether those people are staff, clients, or crews we're teamed up with on a job.

I'd been named Canada's Most Admired CEO and was being photographed for a spread in the *Globe and Mail*. When the two-person crew showed up, they wanted to take a picture of me sitting on my desk. I said, "Let's shoot it out in my shop."

They were reluctant—and, frankly, kind of grumpy. I said, "Were you told to shoot it on my desk? Or is that just where you always take these shots?" I told them we were going to make this fun. "You're going to understand who I am and why it's important that you capture everything you should. And I'm going to send you out of here with a present."

I asked them to go stand by their equipment and let us get a shot of them—like they were on a camping weekend. "A picture that you'd post on Instagram."

One of our staff members programmed the image into our CNC machine. It took two hours to set up the machine, and another two hours of cutting. By the time we finished the photo shoot, we had carved out on a piece of microfibre board a big, beautiful portrait of the two crew members, laughing in our shop as they posed with their camera equipment. We held up the finished product proudly.

Emma and Brad, the photo-shoot crew, stared at the cutout in shock. They were blown away. And their mood amplified in the most positive way. Neither had any idea this technology existed, much less that it worked so quickly or gave such detailed results.

Emma asked, "Why did you do this?"

It was obvious to her the cutout had taken my crew quite a bit of effort.

"Energy is everything, my sweet," I told her. "And I could tell from a mile away that you needed a smile."

Emma apologized for their sullen disposition being so obvious. They'd recently done a photo shoot with another CEO, an older man who sat on the edge of his desk for the duration and constantly complained about the photos. She had to call the paper and say, "I don't know how this man wants me to make him look any different, sitting with his legs crossed on his desk." She was deflated.

"Well, you're here at Freshco Family Ranch now, and I appreciate all professionals in the trades, including you. Technically, you are in the trades, you know."

That started a whole other conversation. I'd shown them that not all CEOs are the same, but also that a shop these days is not what you might expect or assume. Trade workshops today contain highly sophisticated technology and machinery. Meanwhile, their photos were so good that we bought a bunch of them and hired them for other shoots.

You see what I did there, right? I brought some unexpected fun to what Emma and Brad had been approaching as just another dreary, boiler-plate corporate assignment. But that fun wasn't pointless. It opened a door (or two) in their minds.

Fun isn't just pranks, games, nicknames, and tech tricks, though. The other thing that makes our employees feel great about themselves and the company is that we give back. It can't be just me, or just the company, giving to a project or cause. It has to be part of the work culture.

With the number of great organizations and causes out there, something will capture the attention of each employee. We work with Habitat for Humanity; Ronald McDonald House; and our own project, the Chris Rennehan Foundation, which you may recall supports young women in the trades. But on top of our corporate philanthropy, Freshco team members are encouraged to take on something personally that will make a difference in the lives of others. When we encourage our entire team to engage in philanthropic projects, as individuals or in groups, it comes back to us tenfold. It has a positive impact on the company, on the organization being supported, and on our staff, both as a team and as individuals.

Oh—and it's the right thing to do.

The culture of fun at Freshco is rich and deep. It covers everyone and everything. It's contagious. Our clients experience something different from the usual robotlike employees they're used to dealing with. They encounter engaged, playful, positive employees who go the extra mile. And who make them laugh.

And for goodness' sake, don't hire me to do a keynote unless you're ready for me to strip down to my "Respectfully Uncensored" T-shirt and hit you in the head with a projectile from my T-shirt launcher.

It'll only hurt until the pain goes away.

16

HUG THE PERSON NEXT TO YOU

few years back, I flew to Dallas to give a keynote speech on women in leadership for a large consulting firm. While there, I was asked if I would observe some of their breakout sessions and provide feedback. No problem, especially given their offer to add another zero to my fee.

That morning, before the sessions, I stopped by Starbucks and got my usual four long shots of decaf espresso. Hey, no judgment. I had to give up the real stuff for fear of my partner locking me out of the house after watching me go from zero to two hundred between 6 and 7 a.m., accompanied by bouts of sweating and loud behaviour.

In any case, my unwired and curious self followed the arrows to Grand Ballroom A-B on the third floor of the hotel where the conference was taking place. I opened the doors carefully, trying not to interrupt the proceedings.

The room was full—and very quiet. There were about fifty tables of ten people each. Most of the tables were filled with people under thirty. Five or so definitely were not—those ones, I guessed, held upper management. Each table was about two-thirds male and one-third female.

A facilitator on stage was explaining the exercise: each table would have twenty minutes to come up with a response to why its group should take the lead at next year's forum. Starting now.

I watched. Everyone stared at the white notepads in front of them, as if staring would magically make the answers appear. People looked fearful of interacting with each other.

The silence held.

I'd seen enough. I walked over to the facilitator and asked if there was a little bit of runoff time, other than the twenty minutes she had given the group.

She greeted me enthusiastically. "Great to see you, Mandy! We are so excited to hear you speak later." Then she frowned. "Why do you ask about the time?"

"I need the mic, or this session is going to die a quick death." She looked shocked, but handed me the mic and took a step back.

I stepped forward and bellowed: "Okay, folks, put your pens down. We need a pulse check." A ripple spread through the room. Confusion, annoyance, curiosity? It didn't matter. They were waking up.

"Now stand up, hug the person next to you, and say, 'Thank you for sitting next to me today.' You have thirty seconds. Go!"

There was movement, but mostly uncertainty, surprise, people looking at each other with WTF in their eyes. Good. Time for another nudge.

"You now have twenty seconds. And if your actions don't look authentic, look out!"

The room erupted into laughter. It was followed by an audible buzz—the buzz of real human contact and connection. They were actually speaking with each other.

"Okay, now sit your asses down. Now that we have some love flowing in this room, progress will follow. You have two minutes to pick the best candidate from your table to talk to all of us. This person will explain to the room why your table made their selection. This talk will be 50 percent of your score. Go!"

I gave them the time countdown in thirty-second increments, just to be annoying. Upper management was on its feet, applauding, encouraging everyone.

"Stop!"

I gave them ten seconds to quiet down.

"Now I am giving you one more minute to discuss, as part of your presentation, why you would want to have drinks with me later. This will make up 25 percent of your score!"

"I know why," came a shout from table eight. "Because you're funny."

"You're disqualified!" I sternly declared. "Ha, ha! Just joking, folks. Okay, your one minute starts . . . Now!"

The facilitator approached me. "Well, this certainly has taken a twist! Is this part of what we hired you to do? And I missed it?"

"No," I told her. "I've been to too many of these events where the goal is to make an impact on your staff, but they end up leaving and saying, 'It was okay.' As leaders, it's our job to motivate them so they can motivate us." I grinned sheepishly to show I understood that I'd just bulldozed into her session. "I hope you don't mind that I pumped things up."

She smiled at me, we hugged, and we let the clock tick down as we waited to see what would come from this troop of young smarty-pants consultants.

People had rolled up their sleeves, pulled their hair back into pony-tails, and some had even removed their shoes. They were laughing as they worked. When it came time for the presentations, each table cheered on its speaker. And their responses to the questions? They were clever, mind-blowing—it was clear there was a reason these up-and-comers had been selected to work for this company. The personality in the room, once they had "permission" to run wild, was palpable and diverse.

One presenter, a woman named Chunhua, stood out. "I was chosen to work here because of my grade point average from Harvard, and because of the business algorithms I have formulated," Chunhua said. She confessed that being very shy in such a professional environment had made it difficult for her to make friends, so she'd always worked more as an individual. Her voice carried. The enormous room was so silent that, in the pauses between her words, you could have heard a dirty carpet come to life.

"Before Mandy took the stage, I knew nobody at my table, and no one was interacting. I had anxiety over how we would complete this challenge as a team. But because Mandy's presence and energy were so *big*, it was like taking a pill filled with excitement, a pill that encouraged us to work together without being judged."

Now, she'd not only spoken with her team members, she wanted to stay in touch with them after the conference. "They are all awesome, and smart in different ways from me." Chunhua spoke clearly, her head held high. "Mandy, we want to have a drink with you later because we want you to meet who we became together in this last half hour. I wear custom slippers that look like shoes because my feet are always cold. That's why I was picked to be our presenter."

My new shy friend Chunhua, whom I nicknamed Cinderella because of the slippers, was unassuming and did not come across as the powerhouse that she was. But just through her disposition and humility, I could see she was a switchboard of brilliance. Speaking with me afterward, she was overwhelmed with gratitude. She'd just needed to find her voice and break out of the corporate box that had told her to shut up, be an analyst, and not talk. I don't know where she is right now, or what she's doing, but I guarantee you she's doing something that's going to benefit the world.

The corporate world has long been sold to young people as the dream career: that beautiful suit and matching handbag, the promotional ladder, jobs glamorized in movies and on TV (all of them white collar, of course). The race to obtain these shiny positions is real. Parents and teachers promote them as the only viable path forward. Money and a sense of belonging give the appeal an extra boost, and the pull of status puts corporate over the top.

But when our innocent up-and-comers land these jobs, the happy glow is fleeting. The "I have arrived" excitement quickly meets reality, and many of those who "made it" to their desired destinations feel like they're suffocating—dying a slow death—because they have been stuffed into the corporate box. The brilliant ideas these potential leaders were excited to share when they were hired are ignored, discouraged even, a cast-iron lid put on any excitement, and their individuality dampened.

They are told what to wear, how to wear it, how to walk, what words are acceptable, and to whom they may speak. Long hours without adequate compensation are the norm. The office view is, in reality, a sea of cubicles containing sad robotic bodies, each hoping to be beckoned to the big table. Yet even if, once treading water in that sea, you know you want something different, how the hell—especially once those massive student-loan payments kick in—do you go back and start again?

I'd love to be enlightened about how money, assets, and perceived power can so easily turn people into complete titheads. And how can these same corporate "leaders" cause bright, educated, young, forward-thinking, potential leaders with the whole world at their fingertips to become reactive, leave-your-own-ideas-home, uniform-wearing, rule-following robots? Does it have anything to do with having enough room on their fancy credit cards that they are followed blindly as they spring for drinks after work? Can two Manhattans or a couple of Cosmopolitans purchased with someone else's credit card brainwash an otherwise intelligent person into dressing a certain way, leaving their personality and values behind, all in the name of corporate America or Corporate Canada? Do the recruiters actually believe their own bullshit?

I'm always interested in what employers look for when they interview candidates. Who do they prefer to hire? Are they looking for someone who tells them what they want to hear as opposed to what they're really thinking? Or do they want someone who is honest, can learn, and has the ability to make them laugh?

I know *my* answer.

My company grew, and grew some more, until finally my in-house controller told me, "Bear, we need an accounting firm with various arms to help us take on our growth—one that can also do our year-end review."

I agreed, and asked who she would recommend. She thought we should give three larger firms each an interview. She lined them up, and they came into Freshco headquarters one by one to make their case.

Ugh, it was brutal. After the second group had presented, I leaned over to my controller and asked, "Are all accountants this stiff and dry?"

Janet St Pierre Jones, now Freshco's chief financial officer, first became my accountant when I was in my twenties. She and I have been working together for nearly two decades. She is a wonderful, loving, and brilliant woman with the sweetest personality and disposition. Her nickname is Kitten, because she purrs around numbers. But we also call her Piranha, because she will eat you alive if you underestimate her abilities.

"Bear," she said, "that's the problem with a lot of these big firms. They expect their people to look and act in a certain manner. They call it 'professional.'"

Sweet Jesus, save me.

I went out for a quick lunch date with my sweetie—a godsend after listening to those accountants—and was headed back to the office, bracing myself for the third interview. Out of the blue, an older Audi swooshed by me. It did a quick and fierce turn into a parking spot and landed half in the bushes, way past the parking line. A guy in his early fifties got out of the vehicle. His glasses hung crooked on the top of his head, one of his shirt tails was untucked, he had a big coffee stain on the left side of his shirt, and, while I didn't check, I'm sure his socks didn't match.

What a piece of work.

"Well, hello Mandy! I'm Nathan!"

He told me the company he was with. This guy was our third interview for the day.

"Right. I know who you are," I said. "And now you're Bushes. Great parking job. Hope you like your new nickname."

We laughed, staring at his car, and then made our way to the boardroom, where the rest of his team had already gathered. They were the complete opposite of him, stiff and impeccably groomed.

Nathan lowered his bent glasses from the top of his head to his nose. "Mandy," he began, "I am not going to waste your time. I can tell you that the size of this account is not going to make me or anyone around this table rich."

His team glared at him. They were not impressed. I was loving this nonverbal communication.

Nathan went on. "But I know something about what you're doing here, and how. I absolutely love who you are as a person, and as a kickass leader, and I'm here to tell you that I am the very best at what I do. I will make sure you are in good hands as you scale your business."

Done.

That quickly, a real, authentic, straight man with crooked glasses got a lesbian business owner to say "yes" to his proposal. The previous two companies had bored the shit out of me with their inside-the-box, tell-her-what-she-wants-to-hear presentations. Bushes was the real deal.

"Bushes," I said, "you're hired! Thank you for being you. There's coffee and cake pops in the fridge." Before leaving, I added, "Please try to get out of my parking lot without hurting anyone, including yourself."

"You've got it, Bear," he said with a wink.

God, how I love intelligent, real people who make the effort in an otherwise constipated world.

Shit stirred, stinks. A couple of years ago, a large firm hired me to do their keynote. Confidentiality doesn't allow me to get more specific, but the event was held at the most outstanding high-end location, with more than two thousand employees in attendance. They came by the busload, and the Bear Squad showed up early to size things up. If I had the money that company spent on that day, I'd gladly burn mine. They'd pulled out all the stops: the music was loud, the surroundings beautiful, the lighting phenomenal.

You could feel the anticipation in the room when "he" was asked to take the stage. "He" was once the global CEO of this massive entity, and all assembled were on the edges of their seats, psyched for his motivational message.

Then he started to talk. It was like Buzz Killington had staked his claim.

Like somebody had wiped away the sweet aroma that meets us at the front door of a bakery.

Like walking ten blocks to stand in line for the best eggs benny and a cold beer on a Saturday morning, and finding the place has just been evacuated because of a rat sighting.

Get the picture?

Now I realize that, at such events, those inhabiting the upper echelons of the organizations are expected to take the microphone and address the staff, at least briefly. But holy crap, for the love of Anabella the pink elephant, I wanted to jump on stage, grab the microphone, and hand this guy my T-shirt launcher plus an arsenal of T-shirts bearing his face and a motivational quote. If you're putting a CEO in front of two thousand young people you've spent thousands of dollars to recruit, and they're talking among themselves because he can't keep their attention, that's on you. Not everyone has to be me, but you have to deliver in a way that has an impact and makes people listen.

I started to fidget in my seat, in sheer pain for wanting to save this guy from himself. Annie reached over and put her hand on my lap.

"Bear, be good. I know it's bad, but you're up in another hour."

Except the hour slogged on. It became two. By then I was staring at the entrance to the bar with longing, dreaming that a neat and finely aged Scotch would miraculously appear in my hand. Dear God, I needed a drink.

There's always a positive, though, and what I did notice was the crowd: it was diverse in every way, which made me happy and told me that this firm's hiring practices were very progressive.

Finally, it was time. My introduction video, which was barely PG content, played. The energy shift was palpable. The place began to light up. Some had heard me speak before. "Feel It Still" was the song I'd chosen to blast over the speakers. I walked onto the stage with my infamous Renne-grin and stared at them until the place was in 747-over-the-Atlantic-at-2-a.m. quiet.

Then I opened my stance, put my hands on either side of my lapel jacket and ripped her open to reveal what God gave me, with the T-shirt caption "Respectfully Uncensored" emblazoned across my torso. The place erupted with clapping and cheering.

Finally, I said, "This room today is filled with what the governing bodies around statistics would call some of the brightest, most intelligent, up-and-coming stars in the country."

They loved that statement.

"But I have a question for you. Are you likeable?"

Mosquito, please pass gas for all to hear in the silence that followed.

I was ready to take my already-stirred shit and put it in 30-degree (Celsius, of course) sunshine for an extra measure of aroma. I proceeded to tell the audience why I'd hired the accounting firm we'd signed onto with Freshco: because of Bushes and his ability to be real, which made him likeable.

What happened when I finished my keynote was truly triumphant in the world of soft-skill adaptation for a group of geniuses in the making. Many of them approached me, gave hugs, and said, "I don't know if I'm likeable, but I sure hope I am."

But the corporate machine—in fact, it would seem, our whole society—is too clogged to loosen up that easily.

A few days later, one of the firm's employees wrote a global blog about being likeable. My inbox exploded with requests for me to teach people how to be likeable. That was sad for me.

The following week, the company's VP asked me for Bushes' real name so they could thank him formally—for being real and likeable.

Interestingly enough, *Harvard Business Review* has done many studies—I could have given them the answers free of charge, with a bonus Bear hug—which not only suggest but also confirm that only 2 percent of success is explained by IQ. Far more is based on personal intelligence. Personal intelligence is the ability to use one's personality and personal information to problem solve, make plans, and generally contribute to life.

Folks in the blue collar world don't give a shit about all the white collar hoopla. The culture and thought processes in the trades are just the opposite: blue collar people think others should want to be in the trades not because it fits some supposed standard of "success," but because it's beyond rewarding. The blue collar industry is filled with human beings who provide all of life's essentials. They have no desire to be stuck in a takeout container. They want to be in a cooler full of sandwiches, cold beer, and other treats, and they'll pack their own lunch, thank you.

Part of the problem is, when it comes to the trades, we are the poorest marketers in the world. We don't know how to market ourselves because we have never felt you should have to market something so great.

The corporate world, in contrast, damn well knows that the best marketer wins. For decades, the white collar world has been selling corporate culture because the people in that environment know they have to prove they are worthy. They have to throw money at marketing to make it look enticing. They remind me of snake oil salesmen.

My work with Fortune 500 and other brilliant companies has shown me that there are a lot of great white collar folks—and even great corporate leaders. But there are too many who aren't. In my world, companies grow when they let the great ideas of their people be part of the company culture. It's time to give the corporate world a complete enema, and I'm not afraid to say I'm the laxative that is going to get things moving in the right direction.

17

BLUE COLLAR NEEDS ITS OWN PRIDE MOVEMENT

Y ou're crazy, crazy cute. But people like you, and people like me, will never have a relationship."

It took me a moment to process what I was hearing. But the message was loud and clear: the maintenance world was dirty. And by virtue of association, so was I.

I had just landed a $150,000 job with Canada Post. At the ripe old age of twenty, that was huge. My team and I headed out for a celebratory night in the city. Even back then, Halifax was a melting pot of diversity, and being in the midst of so many people who didn't care about what I did for a living—or who I was sleeping with—energized me.

We found a great little place in the heart of downtown Halifax. The Seahorse Tavern, a.k.a. Mandy's playground for the evening, was the quintessential "this is where big names get started" venue: dark and crowded, with an unending parade of musicians hoping to be discovered. During future visits, I would see icons such as Sarah McLachlan, The Tragically Hip, and a host of others perform on that stage. Back then, those up-and-coming artists were hustling for the gigs that would bring them to the big time, just as the rest of us were doing in our fields. It was a place to feel at home on the cusp of possibility, drinking to your dreams as you plotted how to make them real.

My team and I passed the scrutiny of the big, bald bouncer and elbowed our way to a table.

Then, in she walks. I'll never forget the sight. She appeared to be a few years older than me, piercing blue eyes, jet black hair in a stylish bob, with a London Fog–inspired trench coat tied neatly at her tiny waist (excuse me while I imagine what lay beneath). She sat at the bar, and my body walked toward her before my head realized what I was doing. Trying to look calm with a side of charming, I ordered a round of drinks for my table. But my insides were doing backflips. My brain felt like it was in a blender with an electrical short.

Buying her a drink would be a good conversation starter. Nervous as a porcupine on an eight-lane highway, I slid the drink toward her. I rested my forearm on the bar, gave her my best Bear smile, and said something about it being a good Friday.

"Really?" She tilted her head and smiled just enough to make my knees vibrate. "Why don't you tell me about it?"

I froze. I hadn't thought about what I'd do if she responded. Breathe, Mandy. Act normal. Okay. I told her I was with friends, and she said that if I wanted to tell her my story, she'd be there waiting for me. My heart was pounding. Holy what-the-heck-do-I-do-next shit! So I spent an obligatory bit of time with my team, then made my way back to the bar and sidled up beside this captivating woman.

She was from England, doing part of her thesis at one of the local universities. My gut told me she wasn't going to share much about herself. I even sensed that something was a little off, but the details of her life or her inner self, truth be told, weren't, at that moment, my main concern. We had three or four drinks, and the next thing I knew, we were snuggling up in the back seat of a cab, heading over to her parents' summer home, a beautiful condo overlooking the harbour.

We spent the weekend together. All of it. The only time I wandered outside of those four walls was to get us McDonald's—twice. Let's call those Golden Arches meals sustenance—well earned—and leave it at that.

This woman and I had deeply lustful chemistry. It was intoxicating, overwhelming. We had some great conversations, laughed, enjoyed each other's company. I was on a high.

Then she asked what I did for a living. I proudly explained the world of maintenance, how it worked, and the great news I'd just received on the contract. I also told her about my new residential love—a house I'd just purchased on Welsford Street.

At first, I thought her "mmm-hmm" responses were meant to encourage me to share more. But it became clear she was growing bored, so I changed the subject, so to speak. By now, my "something isn't right" bells were ringing like a firehouse drill, but, once again, I pushed those thoughts aside. I was enjoying myself too much.

It was Sunday night, and I'd have to leave early in the morning to drive to Truro, an hour from Halifax, where I was doing a job. I looked into that beautiful face, excited about the possibilities that lay ahead, and asked when we could get together again. After what I considered a frigging awesome couple of days, it couldn't be soon enough for me. Surely, she must feel the same way.

She looked me straight in the face and told me how cute and charming I was. Then she said, "But people like you, and people like me, will never have a relationship."

Full stop.

My stomach flipped again—not in a good way. Had she really just said that? What the actual fuck? I could get past her not wanting to see me again for any number of reasons, but the meaning behind her words was deep and ugly to me. What she was saying was, an academic, especially one with money, couldn't be with "just" a maintenance worker.

In that single moment, she went from being what I thought was my dream girl—beautiful, smart, exciting, fun, and sexy as hell—to someone I couldn't get away from fast enough. The physical attraction died on the spot. She had used me for sex, but I wasn't good enough to date. I certainly wasn't relationship material, given my chosen profession.

That experience could have ruined my future—if I'd let it. I see people walk away from their dreams all the time because of someone else's perception of which dreams are worthy. But no way was I letting her stuck-up, closed-minded attitude cut me down. I was hurt—devastated, actually—but that only pushed me harder. That experience lit a fire in me.

It didn't take long for me to realize that her rejection of me, though it felt deeply personal, wasn't personal at all, because it's like that with everyone in the trades and maintenance fields. I rejected her backward thinking—her prejudice. The shock of it was as real as the heart attack that would kill my brother at thirty-eight. I was making it in a man's world as a gay female—a huge breakthrough in a still-backward society. Only now I was being judged by the colour of my collar.

I shook off that woman's disdain and, armed with my new Canada Post contract and my rising prospects, proudly, confidently, marched forward to build what is now a multi-million-dollar business that encompasses many trades. And my bottomless disgust and frustration over attitudes like hers eventually led to my Blue Collar CEO work, celebrating the trades and commanding the respect the industry deserves.

A woman approached me after a keynote speech. She was the mother of twins. "I'm a twin!" I told her. Then she shared her story.

"They're identical," she said. Except that one had gone into commerce and the other into electrical work. "My boy in electrical is the personality of the two. But they're both on one of those dating apps, and he gets very few matches because he's in the trades."

The one in commerce was planning to do his PhD because, according to his mother, "he'd rather keep studying than get out and work." The electrician, meanwhile, was doing his apprenticeship, had no debt, and was driven to succeed; but because he was blue collar, most women scrolled right past him.

She was so upset by this she began to cry. And oh, could I feel her pain. And her son's.

When I think back on that hot academic—not so hot anymore— who dismissed me, I figure her book smarts had replaced any common sense she may have once possessed. It was apparent she didn't have the slightest clue that the qualified person who had put those highlights in her hair was a tradesperson. So was the technician who had provided that polished manicure.

I could go a long way with this line of thinking. Who built her vehicle and the intricate transportation system she travelled through every day? Who constructed every single inch of that exquisite condo overlooking the harbour, and who had planned and installed the electrical and plumbing in every building she'd ever been in?

Blue collar professionals had done it all, and without them, she and everyone else on this planet would wake up naked and hungry, in an unmowed field, no shelter, no running water, no plumbing, no transportation—nothing. Every single day.

You're fucking welcome.

I'm forever at a loss to figure out how the guy who goes to university for ten years, becomes an accountant, goes into commerce, and becomes a superstar because he wears a suit and has a piece of paper naming the institution he attended can make $150,000 a year and be called a professional, compared with the guy who built the very fundamentals of everything the first guy uses every day, who is simply considered a "handyman." Call me naive, but I don't think people are born with that type of short-sighted thinking. There has to be something that triggers it—or, in some distorted way, condones it. Generational thinking. Learned behaviour. Sadly, this backward way of thinking is rampant in North America, and it's embedded in some people like a hungry tick in a stinky armpit.

Look at the people who built our countries, our cities, our communities. Everything we see around us, *everything*, was built by astoundingly talented people who were, and are, treated like second-class citizens because the work they do is seen as dirty or immaterial. These extraordinary people have gone through schooling, apprenticeship, training, and more to become professionals in their chosen fields. Most are hybrids, experts in more than one field. But to the world, they're "workers," *lowly* workers.

See the steam coming out of my ears as I pull my hair out?!

———

In 2007, my team took on the massive job of retrowelling a retailer's concrete floor, which would take two full weeks of night work while the store was closed. I had a team that was highly educated for this type of process and who I knew would do the job to my standards, so I didn't have to be hands-on. I was in my hotel room. At 10 p.m., the job lead, Andrew, called me.

"Mandy, the manager won't let us in the store."

"Why the hell not?"

He told me again that the manager just wouldn't let the team in. I asked Andrew if he'd been clear about what company they were with.

"I don't think she likes the way I'm dressed," he finally said.

I drove to the store, where I found two women, cashier and manager, behind the counter. When the manager came to the door, I told her my name and explained that I was with Freshco. She let me into the shop. I asked her how things were going, and she told me they were great. Her name was Tammy.

"I understand your floor's getting fixed—whole new retrowel."

"Yes," she replied, obviously excited.

"Do you know what goes into that job, Tammy? Only a certain type of person is trained to do this type of work. There are five guys out there, professionals, ready to start the job, but you've refused to let them into the store to get started. Am I missing something? Did one of my guys say something inappropriate to you? What is the issue?"

Tammy looked a bit embarrassed. "Mandy, it was just the way they were dressed. I didn't feel comfortable."

"They're dressed in overalls and workboots and look like white cement because that's what they do. And I assure you they work under me, and you'll never meet nicer, or more professional, people.

I'd appreciate it if we could just forget that a judgment happened here tonight, and you let these men in to do the job that you hired us to do."

Tammy apologized and asked how she could remedy the situation. I invited her to watch the process for a while.

"But Tammy, it'll take the team about fifteen minutes to get set up, so maybe you can go to the Tim Hortons down the street and bring them each back a coffee and a donut."

She was back in less than fifteen minutes.

Educating people on the importance of the trades is one way to effect change. Chatting with Tammy, helping her understand why she shouldn't judge as she had, made a difference. She apologized profusely. I had protected my team, been their voice and their shield, although I can never protect my team against everything the ignoramuses of the world throw at them.

Let's be honest. I could have told Tammy that she was just the manager of a retail store. But people in the trades don't tend to be judgmental.

The repercussions of not treating our tradespeople like the true professionals they are isn't just that it demeans them. That's bad enough. We've also created a massive supply-and-demand issue in the trades industry. Brilliant minds and talent won't even consider the trades because of this bullshit perception.

That has to be remedied now, or even the status quo will fall by the wayside, thrusting us backward at a pace that will kick our collective asses back a century. We are already on that disturbing trajectory. Good luck finding a qualified tradesperson to fix your dishwasher or a leaky toilet, much less someone to build a new home. This insidious issue is now full blown, in our faces, and affecting everything we do. We've created a shortage of skilled trades in Canada and the United States so critical that we won't be able to maintain the infrastructure we have, much less build an economy that relies on modernized building standards. People, we're in a shitload of trouble.

I sit on panels with the likes of Microsoft and Amazon, and I work with various government agencies and departments. I asked a recent panel, "Okay, boys and girls, when's the last time you called someone to fix your dishwasher?"

They just stared at me. The one guy who was willing to be vulnerable enough to respond laughed and said, "My wife and I have been waiting for two weeks for this guy to come from across the city, because he's the only one who fixes this type of dishwasher and he's so busy. No one else fixes this brand. When he gets there, he'll need a part; that's another two weeks."

I replied, "Does it not seem a bit odd that you have the money to pay someone to fix your dishwasher, a common efficiency, and, to be quite frank, something that makes your life easier, but you can't find anyone to fix it?"

The looks on their faces usually tells me they've never given this question much thought. And that is part of the problem. Whatever thought they do give the guy who fixes their dishwasher more often than not has to do with what it costs—and a knee-jerk belief that he's charging more than he's worth.

The gentleman next to me on a recent flight struck up a conversation. We discussed our respective professions and properties in Florida.

"Have you heard of SharkBites?" he asked.

"Yes," I said. "And they should be illegal. Anyone using them in my company gets fired. They're a shortcut, and we don't do half-ass work."

SharkBites are U-shaped fittings used in plumbing to connect various pipes, replacing soldering. The issue with these fittings is that, with different levels of pressurized water, there is a high probability the "shortcut" will either cause a leak or blow. Some plumbers use them—the lazy ones who don't care about their profession.

My seatmate told me his pipes had blown out in the bathroom late at night. His wife, who was home alone, called the plumbing company down the street. They came to the house, cut the wall out to find the leak, fixed it, and saved them from a flood.

"That's awesome!" I replied. I love it when the pros show up and do their thing.

"But look at the bill," he said, pulling up his invoice on his laptop.

I didn't think it was any of my business, but he asked. So I took a peek. The total was thirteen hundred dollars.

"Do you want me to tell you what I think?" I asked. I knew exactly where he was going, and I was about to give him a reality check.

"Please, Mandy," he said.

"So, I just want to recap," I said. "Your wife is alone in the home. The pipes start bursting inside the walls of your brand-new house. She calls the company. They're there within forty-five minutes, with three technicians, at 11 o'clock at night. They not only fixed the problem, but they stopped any greater damage from happening. They even put drying equipment there for when you're ready to start rebuilding. And you think thirteen hundred dollars is gouging?"

I tried to be calm, but I was pissed.

"I thought the bill was really high."

"Respectfully, you need to give your fucking head a shake. When you got your bill from the lawyer who did the closing on your home indicating that between him and his secretary, they may have put a total of two hours into the whole deal, and the bill was for twice this much, did you even think about it?"

"Well, if you put it that way—"

"Why is it that a professional—at least a pro by society's definition—can put any price tag on their services and are never questioned? But a professional in the trades leaves his warm bed and his family to come out at 11 fucking o'clock at night, stays on the job until the problem is solved, charges an overtime rate of $125 an hour—which is still three hundred dollars less than what your lawyer charges—and he's gouging?"

I told this gentleman I didn't understand.

"You know, Mandy, I just learned that I shouldn't poke the Bear next to me. And, second, duly noted. You are absolutely right. Lesson learned."

"Oh, I know I'm right. These three men made sure your wife was safe in her home despite the flooding. They even called her back the next day to make sure she was okay, and to check that the drying machines hadn't tripped a breaker. They told her how she could fix it if they did."

Compensation in the trades industry *is* lucrative, and entrepreneurship and trades go hand in hand. What I'm still fighting with my movement to redefine the collar blue is that people think a plumber at seventy dollars an hour is highway robbery but think nothing of paying a hundred fifty dollars for their first visit to get orthotics. You don't call the "orthotics man" at midnight if your feet hurt. You wait. But you do call your plumber, and he comes—or, in some cases, she comes.

My seatmate's fear that he was being overcharged wasn't completely out of left field. As in any profession, there are tradespeople—like the ones who'd installed less than high-quality plumbing in his new house—who do shoddy work and still charge a fortune. This is the other side to there not being enough good contractors (because there isn't enough respect of the trades to lure enough good people to these careers): regardless of skill level, contractors can jack up their prices. So goes the law of supply and demand. It's happening to me as a consumer, too. I'm getting ripped off with the rest of the world.

We need more people in the trades.

One of the ways I've tried to nudge people toward a new perspective on tradespeople and their exceptional range of skills is to look at Leonardo da Vinci. A polymath, academic, and artist, he could fix just about anything and create even more. That is exactly what I see when I look at our uncles, fathers, neighbours: the many and varied skill sets that mean, with one call for help, our repair and maintenance issues are whisked away. (Funny side note: I've been referred to as Bear Vinci more than once.)

It's one thing for a trade itself not to have respect (wrong on every count), but when it spills over onto the tradesperson, that is another story. I've had many, many conversations with people in different trades, and the conversation is usually the same.

I tell them how impressive their work is, and they respond with shock and embarrassment. "Well," they'll say, "I'm only a plumber."

Blue collar professionals don't do what they do for the accolades, and, frankly, history has taught them not to look for them.

I reply, "You're more than that to me. You're one of the smartest, most fastidious professionals I've ever seen."

"No one's ever called me a professional," they'll tell me, often with an uncomfortable laugh.

It's difficult to take a compliment or see the good in yourself when you've been put in a box your whole life. It's maddening watching folks look around as if they'll be arrested for impersonating a real professional. We've created that, and we can *un*create it. Perception is everything. It can crush or create. It can inspire or cripple. It can divide people or bring them closer together.

The power we have to educate others on the trades, and the difference it will make, really hit home when I walked away with Canada's Most Admired CEO award and the CEOs of both McDonald's and WestJet approached me. They wanted me to know they appreciated me and the trades. That mattered. The WestJet guy said, "Rennehan, shit, you're funny. Too bad you're not into airplanes."

I told him I was glad to fly around on them, but I had other work to do.

Even more meaningful to me were the cameramen, waiters, and caterers at the banquet, all grabbing my hand and saying thank you.

"Mandy, finally someone recognizes what we do."

Afterward, at the restaurant in the Shangri-La Hotel, Annie and I walked by a tableful of women. I had no idea who they were, but one of them grabbed my hand. "Thank you," she said, tears in her eyes. "Thank you, Mandy. We are all in our forties and saw you at the awards banquet. For the first time, you made us feel wonderful about what we do for a living."

These weren't just words they were sharing. I could feel the shift in these valuable humans. Someone simply had to give them permission to shine.

18

THINK YOU'RE TOUGH?
THINK AGAIN

In Yarmouth and other seafaring towns throughout Nova Scotia, we have what's referred to as "dumping day." It takes place at the end of November, on the first day of the lobster-fishing season, when our fishermen head out with their vessels loaded down with traps to be laid out in hopes that, when hauled back up, they'll be stuffed with lobster.

The community gathers along the shoreline at 5 a.m., bundled up in winter garb to ward off the biting cold. There's nary a complaint, as we know our circumstances onshore are nothing compared with what our fishermen are about to experience. Hot coffee, bread pudding, and warm muffins are passed around. There is a blessing of the fleet and prayers for those heading out. Then the boats parade out to sea, one by one, vessel headlights shining in the darkness.

It's damned difficult to articulate the feeling in the air on that once-a-year morning. Those gathered onshore don't say much, but they're all gripped by a potent blend of anxiety and hope. So are the fishermen. They know an entire region's economy depends on their catch, and they're headed out to risk their lives to get it.

As a family, we didn't sit around the kitchen table and talk about Pup's profession every time he ventured out to sea. But we were thankful every night he came home safely, because there were never any guarantees that he would.

When I was young, somewhere between eight and twelve, I went out fishing with Pup a few times. It was exciting for a kid, and a big deal to work alongside the guys. I had no idea what fishing was like on a rough day, because Pup took me out only on the calm ones. Onboard, he kept a supply of Hubba Bubba and Popeye bubble gum, bought from our local candy store, Toots. Chewing it kept me from getting sick.

Years later, when I was in my early twenties, I decided to come home for a visit. The truth is, I wanted to be back in Pup's world for a bit, to get that feeling again, because there's nothing quite like being on the sea. Given what I had been through businesswise the past few years, I figured I could handle a day or two on the water.

Waking up at 3:30 in the morning was the first indication that I may have forgotten just how tough the job was. But I dragged myself out of bed, ready to go.

"It looks like it's gonna be a pretty good day out there, dear," Pup said, over our quick breakfast.

Bernie was his captain, and Donald was his partner in crime on the stern of the boat. They were already at the wharf when Pup and I arrived, as were lots of other fishermen. The aroma of pipe tobacco was in the air, and everybody had their truck lights on because it was, after all, the middle of the night. Donald hauled out a big machete and, pipe hanging from one side of his mouth, started chopping the fish heads off for the bait bags that would go into the pots. Pup was getting the rope ready and prepping the barrels for the catch.

Then it was all aboard, and we went chugging away from the relative safety of the wharf. The low-key, down-to-business rumble of a real fishing boat never leaves your mind once you've heard it.

Imagine heading out to sea just as the sun starts to peek over the horizon. It's a breathtaking scene, and you're part of it. That particular day we were fishing off of what was referred to as "the gully." I didn't know, at first, the significance of this. Pup and the crew were hauling up pots, and Bernie was in the captain's chair. My job was to band the lobsters, the process of putting thick rubber bands around their claws. I'd measure their backs and band the ones big enough to keep. The rest would be thrown back into the ocean. I donned my oil clothes and I was feeling good about everything. I had a smile on my face.

Until I didn't. All of a sudden, the wind picked up out of the north, then out of the northwest, a fisherman's nightmare if it gets too strong.

Pup told me, "Dear, did I forget to tell you? We're fishing in the gully now, which means there's a lot of swell on the seas. We're gonna rock 'n' roll for the rest of the day. But that's okay, dear. You're okay. You've been out here before."

I think he was trying to talk me into being okay, because he had a pretty good sense of what was coming.

Then it hit me. Even without a mirror, I knew my face was turning an ugly shade of green. My stomach started turning, which was something I'd never experienced on the water before. Pup kept checking back with me, a little grin on his face.

"How you feeling, dear?" he'd ask every few minutes.

"I'm fine, Pup," I'd report back.

"You can go down in the cud if you need to."

"No," I'd tell him. "I'm feeling fine."

Donald was keeping an eye on me, too, and he said something in French. Dad wasn't bilingual by any stretch of the imagination, but he had fished so long with Donald that he knew exactly what he was saying. They both had a chuckle but continued on with their business and left me to mine, partly, I'm sure, to keep my pride intact.

About half an hour later, I couldn't hold it any longer, and I started woofing my guts up over the side. Now picture it: the boat is rocking in the ocean swells, and there's nothing really to hang onto when you're doubled over the side puking. Dad was holding onto everything from my oil gear to my bloomers, making damn sure I didn't go overboard.

Holy shit, I've never been that sick.

The guys grabbed an old rag, dipped it in the ocean, which continued to come up to meet us, and put it in front of me. It was apparently my washcloth, for wiping the puke off my face.

I got through it. It wasn't pretty, but I thought, *Okay, I've been sick, so now I should be fine.* Turns out that was nothing but wishful thinking. We were heading even farther offshore for the next haul. It was about 10:30 in the morning and, according to the boys, time for a quick break. It turned out Pup and Donald had tuna and baloney sandwiches. They started removing the waxed paper from their sandwiches, and that was all it took to send me scrambling down to the cud and headfirst into the toilet.

I was rolling back and forth with the boat, hands on both sides of that nasty toilet, dry heaving like there was no tomorrow.

All I could think was, *Bear, you think you're tough? Think again.*

At one point, when I came up out of the cud looking like death had just slapped me in the face, Donald said with a sly smile, "I always remember Mandy being tough as her old man."

And at that moment, I'm sure what they saw was sheer admiration on my face. Not only for Dad, but for Donald and the whole crew. This was apparently a calm day, and I was so sick I couldn't function or think straight. I knew what I had to do.

"Bernie," I said. "Off the record, if you'll bring me to shore, whatever you catch today, I'll double it. I don't care, I'll double it."

He looked me straight in the face and calmly said, "Mandy, them's not the rules." They would have to pull all the pots they had laid before heading back. "You'll have to get comfortable with that, because what you want is not happening."

And now, Pup and the boys started laughing their arses off. I wasn't dying. I was just seasick. Very seasick. And they were making the most of it.

When I finally got back to shore, I had a whole new perspective on what "tough" meant, and how holy-shit-amazing our fishermen are.

The lobster fishery is brutal, and it goes a hell of a lot deeper than throwing a trap overboard and hoping for the best. The science of fishing lobster is executed from out on the Atlantic, in some of the roughest conditions and coldest waters known to humanity.

Yet my father said to me one day, not too long ago, "Mandy, I was a lobster fisherman for almost forty years and nobody, until they knew you were my daughter, called me 'Sir.' Nobody ever held the door open for me and nobody called me 'Mr. Rennehan.'"

It took a lot for Pup to share that with me. And it still gives me an awful hollow feeling in the pit of my stomach. He's a very proud man. His words came from a place of hurt.

As a fisherman in a small community, my father wasn't known by many people outside a small sphere. But that's changed. Pup works for me now: I couldn't watch him work his arse off and risk his life in the fishing industry any longer. It took a desperate toll on him and on the entire family.

Now he helps me out with my business—he has for years. Many tradespeople don't feel it's their job to clean up after themselves: that's always been a pet peeve of mine. It's one of the reasons things get scratched or damaged, tools go missing, you've got dents on your floors. Pup is a jack of all trades who's always taken care with his equipment and his worksites: he couldn't afford to do otherwise. He understands the value of things. So he's been my cleaner and my organizer. When Pup was in his fifties and sixties, I flew him to job sites all over the country: he would make sure those sites were straight and tidy, the tools put away at the end of the day. You can't knock his drywalling, either: he's among the best. My entire team appreciates him.

Yet he keeps telling me, "Dear, nobody ever sees the little things I do." Sometimes, how the world has treated us is so ingrained in our being that even when things change, we don't dare accept it, for fear it will disappear or for fear that it's not real.

It's important that Pup knows we see everything he does for my work team and for our family. I bring him to events and make a big deal of him, because he deserves it and, in my own way, I am trying to make up for the hurt others have inflicted on him with their lack of respect. He's my everything. And heads-up, don't insult Pup by saying hello to "Mandy's dad." Instead, call him "Sir," because we all deserve that respect, regardless of what we do for a living or who our family members are.

The world is full of people like Pup, whose skills are overlooked or underestimated, and who aren't always given the respect they deserve. I sat on a panel with an AI (artificial intelligence) expert a short time ago, and I told him right out, "You'll never meet an algorithm like my old man."

Of course, I also tease Pup mercilessly and tell him he doesn't do a damn thing for us. It keeps him humble and on his toes, and we laugh about it. In the end, Pup is two things to me: my real hero and an absolute pain in the ass.

19

GOOD MAINTENANCE ALSO MEANS ADDRESSING YOUR OWN "PAIN POINTS"

I was so overcome, the woman hosting our visit asked sharply, "Are you okay?"

She was concerned, but I doubt she was surprised. The CEO of Ronald McDonald House Charities Canada, she was giving my staff and me a tour through a Ronald McDonald House, a "home away from home" near the hospital where families of sick children could stay. We saw tired parents preparing meals in the central kitchens, and others playing with or reading to young children who were obviously fighting for their lives. Regardless of their circumstances, the parents all exhibited an air of gratitude. I could see how much it mattered that a place like this one existed to help ease their burden as they struggled through what was probably the most difficult period of their lives.

Walking through a Ronald McDonald House, you can't help but be affected, not only by the comfortable facilities and the awe-inspiring staff and volunteers, but also by the fact that you and your family are not in this same situation at the moment. That this type of support exists for those who need it most is so moving, it could overwhelm even the toughest person's emotions. But in my case, though I felt the power of this place and what it offered to families in crisis, there was something else going on—something personal.

It was 2017. My team and I were there because Katrina White, my strategist at the time (we called her BSE, for Bear's Strategy Expert), had introduced me to a senior vice-president with McDonald's. BSE felt strongly that our philanthropic and business values would align nicely, and she was correct.

After speaking with me a few times, the vice-president had told me he was convinced I would find the partnership I was looking for with the Ronald McDonald organization, one that would include all my Freshco staff in a meaningful way. My staff would be able to take ownership of projects throughout Canada and the United States. Each staff member would "own" a Ronald McDonald House, taking responsibility for its regular maintenance, and any minor remodels that needed doing. By doing work at cost and in-house, and by using the technicians we deal with daily to get in front of problems, we could save each home a significant amount on work orders. And our staff would know they were helping this truly remarkable organization and the families it supports. He arranged for us to meet with their CEO at a nearby location. She could show us how it all worked.

As we finished the tour, we walked by an old photo of a Ronald

McDonald House from the 1970s. Seeing it, I caught my breath. The change in me was immediate and intense. My emotions swelled. I was shaken.

It had come back to me, all in a rush: when I was eleven years old and in 4-H, I'd been part of a public-speaking contest, and my topic had been the Ronald McDonald houses. How was it that I'd had several conversations with representatives of the organization, thought deeply about its fit with Freshco, walked through a Ronald McDonald House, and was only now making the connection? It was a classic case of what I call CRS: Can't Remember Shit. We can all relate. Your brain is so overloaded with the present—work stuff, family stuff, you name it—you lose access to parts of your past, or there's the sense of some memory being just out of reach. It's like a constant pinch from the most annoying person in the world.

Glancing at that photo had immediately reversed my CRS.

By this time, as a company, Freshco was well known for its ability to quickly fix any pain points. "Pain points" are irregular problems companies need sorted out—and we love a challenge. We've been referred to as the problem solvers inside the world of facilities. Not every issue has an obvious fix-it algorithm or a "how to" booklet, so we swoop in. There is a "wow" moment with every crisis we solve, and building partnerships is the bonus to our work.

The idea, of course, was to bring this particular Freshco magic to the Ronald McDonald houses, to help make their managers' lives easier. But this sudden memory of my 4-H speech had brought one of my own persistent "pain points" rushing to the surface. The day I was to give that speech, I'd been in a state of panic. Not because I was nervous.

Because my pants didn't fit.

Crystal Hilton, one of my wonderful 4-H leaders, had a knack for recognizing talents in kids and drawing them out. One year, when the 4-H public-speaking contest was coming up, she came to me and said, "Mandy, you're a great speaker, with a great personality. You need to do this."

I trusted Crystal, but I was dubious. "What am I going to talk about?"

I remember wondering if this was just another challenge I could overcome in the long list of 4-H challenges. Would it be like training a calf for show, learning how to be the best partner on a cross-cut saw, pulling with my team in a tug of war contest?

"No idea what you could talk about," she said, with that twinkle in her eye. "But give me a day to figure that out."

The very next day, Crystal bounced up beside me and declared, "Ronald McDonald houses."

I smiled back at her, grateful as usual to be in her presence. But I hoped she had more information to share, because the entirety of what I knew about Ronald McDonald consisted of buying Big Macs on my first school trip to Halifax. It was like the second coming of you know who when, in 1985, the morning of that trip, Ma gave me twenty bucks—enough to allow me to eat enough to get sick off of everything on the McDonald's menu. Of course, with that money, I also had to manage to bring each of my family members a combo meal. From three hours away, it wasn't the best idea, but because we didn't have the famous McD's in our little town, it was a huge deal. The fact that my classmates and I lived to see the next day, what with the lethal flatulent activity on that poor yellow can throughout the bus ride home, was truly a miracle.

What else did I know about Ronald McDonald? I knew he was a clown and a mascot. Not exactly award-winning speech material.

But a little research solved that. It turned out there was a lot of information on Ronald McDonald houses and the phenomenal work they do, and even back in the eighties, with no Google, it was easy to come by.

I practised and practised and practised that speech until I could do it in my sleep. The big day came. I rolled out of bed, padded across the floor to my pile of laundered clothes in the corner, and started to get dressed. That was when it happened.

I went into the kitchen, shoulders down, looked at Ma, and said, in a very self-controlled panic, "My pants don't fit."

The panic was real. I had this speech that I had practised, a theatre full of people with expectations, a contest to hopefully win—and for a kid, that was a lot. My angst had nothing to do with getting up in front of people. Heck, I was born to be in front of a crowd. But I needed pants. Right away. That fit.

Ma glanced quickly at the clock on the wall, grabbed the car keys, and took off for Frenchy's, our local thrift store. There was no money to buy something new. She came back in record time, with three pairs of pants slung over her arm. She rolled the cuffs up on the only pair that fit me—a pair that I hated—and handed them over to me with her "crisis averted and don't argue with me" look.

"Now, Mandy, I know you're not happy with this. It's the best I can do. And come hell or high seas, you're getting out there on that stage and you're doing that speech."

"I am not!"

I was in tears, and pissed off beyond words.

Ma was usually very passive, but she looked me straight in the face and said, "You are. And I'm going to be watching."

She was right on both counts. When I stepped onto the stage of our local theatre to give my speech in those godawful pants, she was there, front and centre, with a big, nervous smile on her face. I remember thinking that it was the first time my mother had truly shown empathy for me. She didn't make a habit of coming to my sporting or school events. I'll never forget seeing her in the audience that morning. I was eleven years old, and my mother was watching me.

In her own way, Ma was willing me to forget about the pants and focus on doing what I was made to do. She was right. Public speaking was one of the many prodigious skills I learned through the 4-H program, and I picked it up way more quickly than, say, training a calf. Who knew that speaking in front of crowds would come so naturally to me, or that it would later become so important in my professional life? I won the contest, and I got to travel throughout Canada delivering my Ronald McDonald House speech to other communities. It was a mind-blowing experience.

But try as I might, I could not forget those damn pants. I still can't. I hated them because they were catfish ugly, and I hated them even more because I knew I couldn't wear clothes like the other kids did, because my body just wasn't having it. Ma felt helpless because, for the life of her, she could not figure out how her athletic kid, who was always on the go, could be so thick—size-wise, that is.

Years later, when it all came rushing back as I stood looking at that old photo on the wall of a Ronald McDonald House, it wasn't the pride that surfaced, but the panic.

The problem was, my pants still didn't fit. And a lot more besides.

—

Fast forward. Something was seriously off. I'd ended up in outpatients eight times within a six-month period, with what I thought were heart attack symptoms.

It turned out it wasn't my heart. Instead, I was having panic attacks so severe I thought I was dying with each one. So much so, that I repeatedly told Sara, who was my partner then, "You know where my will is, and you know the decisions I want you to make."

The little pills the doctor had given me were amazing. Slip one of those under my tongue and, within half an hour, I was fine. It's no damn wonder people become addicted to these drugs. If I could go from discussing my will to "I'm fine" in thirty minutes, that was some pretty powerful stuff.

Still, I was troubled, and puzzled, by these attacks. I'd never experienced anything like them. I reached out to my friend who was a medical doctor and told her my concern. Yes, my life was hectic and stressful, but these attacks were coming out of nowhere, and my inability to control them felt like a death sentence.

I told the doctor I'd done a time-stamp of when I started having the panic attacks. After finishing a home renovation job, we had a sales showing. Earlier, we'd used a piece of heavy equipment to move some large stones on the property, but there was still a huge rock in a spot I didn't like: it looked awkward for the photo shoot, sitting there in the backyard. I decided to fix it. I rolled this heavy stone a couple of metres myself—using my legs and shoulders.

At first, I felt nothing. Then I started getting an excruciating pain in my middle back and sternum, and my ribcage was on fire.

The doc thought it might be a muscle or nerve issue, and she ordered an MRI.

She called the next day to tell me they could get me in for the test in a couple of months but would reach out if there was a cancellation. I politely thanked her and put the phone down. But I wanted to scream.

Do not get me started on the pitfalls of a socialized health system. I know it's free, and we are one of the luckiest nations on earth because of that. But the system is a slow one, and I needed tests done right away so I could continue to run my company. Waiting would be devastating, financially and otherwise.

The following day, fully realizing my privilege, I was in Buffalo, slapping my credit card down in a capitalist-system health centre. I had test results within twenty-four hours. My MD friend called me into her office to discuss the results. I had two herniated disks and costochondritis, which meant—brace yourself—the ripping of my sternum tissue.

Ugh.

She told me that based on the radiologist's reading, there was compression on my spine. Together with all the inflammation surrounding my ribcage, this condition was completely indicative of panic attacks.

Now we were getting somewhere.

"What's the solution, doc?"

"That's where it gets tricky."

Apparently there is no treatment for costochondritis. And I might need surgery for my back.

Relaying that tidbit of information to someone like me wasn't easy, I'm sure. I left her office feeling deflated. I went home and poured a very strong drink. Sara and I had to discuss the options. I couldn't live with panic attacks *or* frequent trips to outpatients. It was killing me slowly. Yet surgery seemed outrageous—they'd be opening me up and going into my spine—and there was no guarantee it would help. There was even some risk it would cause more problems. Sara, with her kinesiology and nutrition background, believed we could cure this naturally, with diet, acupuncture, chiropractic treatments, and facilitated stretching. "There is no way they're operating on your back," she told me. "It's not happening."

Other practitioners we knew and consulted, from osteopaths to chiropractors, agreed. They all said I would never be perfect, but that I could definitely fix a lot of this on my own. With some hard work and discipline, that is.

And time. Trying to cure this organically would take time, and that was something I wasn't quite sure I could deal with. But Sara was right: I had to try. I felt like I had fire hoses turned on me from every direction, pummelling me hard.

For one thing, Freshco was on fire—in a good way—growing so fast that for me to step back for any length of time, would, I felt, be disastrous. We were dealing with potholes full of issues in the United States, from accounting nightmares with the IRS (don't get me started) to dealing with all the different regulations in the various states where my company did work. I had two custom homes on the go plus a complete renovation of our Canadian office.

Meanwhile, it was as if my entire family was falling apart. It was 2007. We were still reeling from Chris's death the previous year. His wife, Simone, was working around the clock to make ends meet. Their sons, my nephews, were both struggling with the loss of their father—one barely left the house and the other was falling in with a bad crowd. My twin, Trev, had separated from his wife and seemed to be falling into a depression. My older brother, Troy, was on a dangerous spiral as a result of his alcoholism: his partner had left him, and he was now living with Ma. Just Ma. Because, to top it all off, Ma and Pup, now in their sixties, had separated.

No one could have prepared me for what life would be like dealing with my parents after they split up. There was no helpline I could call for the challenges I was facing. Meanwhile, there were instant and real financial concerns: as my business had grown, I'd begun helping to support my parents in a serious way. I would now need to provide two of everything: houses, vehicles, phones, laptops, and a host of other necessities. Add to that, with them being separated, I would spend double the time making sure that, emotionally, they were each surviving this radical change in their lives.

I'd felt responsible for my parents' happiness as a kid twenty-five years before, and now that I was an independent adult with a successful career, I felt even more responsible.

In the midst of all this, Troy's situation worsened. He was out West, where he'd gone to work in the oil fields—only he'd never made it to the job. From a distance, I tried to come to his aid in a way that was not going to further his downward spiral but, instead, would help him reverse it. My attempt necessitated a kind of tough love that was wrenching to wield. It meant saying "no" when, in my heart, I wanted to say "yes." It meant a phone call that made me feel like I was turning my back on my brother. I knew that the kind of help he wanted from me, if I were to give it, would only serve to keep him going down a road that would lead to more heartache, for him and for us. So I told him I loved him, and I told him where in his community he could turn for help. Then, feeling as if my heart was being torn out of my chest, I hung up.

The thing is, when we talk about resiliency in business, we also talk about the resilience of your heart. I didn't know that my mind could ever speak to my heart in that regard: that I would ever be able to say "no" like that. But when you're at the point where you've exhausted all avenues of empathy, when you know you're part of the problem, not part of the solution, you have to set that boundary. I knew I could lose him—but I also knew that I couldn't help him anymore. That was something that I had to accept.

That doesn't mean I gave up. Unbeknownst to him, I also contacted a local social service organization. Eventually, thank God, he turned up there seeking help. They let me know. Eight years on, so far, so good. But I didn't know then how things would work out. And I didn't know that finding that strength would prove to remind me, time and time again, that such strength is possible. And that it would help me understand when I see others, friends or staff, struggling with similar situations. At the time, I only knew that I'd come to that boundary, that I had to act, and that things might get worse before they got better, if they ever did.

Then, in 2008, I went to Ottawa to pick up Trev. He was going through such a hard time that I brought him back to live with Sara and me. Eventually, I got Trev set up with a new job at Freshco's head office in Oakville and a place to live in Toronto. I kept tabs on his wife and the boys, trying to help out where and when I could. I went from Ma to Pup and back, trying to make sure they were both settling into their new, solo lives.

Basically, I was going full throttle, trying to sort out everyone's problems but my own.

What else could happen? I'll tell you what. I began getting up in the morning to find that Sara was upset with me. So upset that she would barely speak to me.

I'd ask, "Is everything okay?"

I'd get a glare in return—the most severe stink eye. If she spoke at all, it would be to say, "You can't tell me you don't know."

But I didn't.

Finally, one morning, she told me, "Bear you ripped the sheets off me in the middle of the night!" I'd said cruel things to her—awful, unprintable things. "Your eyes were wide open. Why would you say things like that to me?"

I had no memory of anything except the two of us heading off to bed together, on good terms. The hurt in her eyes was more than I could take. I begged her forgiveness.

But the truth was, this sort of thing had happened before, with previous partners. Once, I'd picked my partner up out of bed because I believed the bed was sinking. Another time, I went into my closet and was beating everything around in there because I thought someone was holding my mother against her will. I've been told at times my language would give a sailor a run for his money.

Eventually, Sara and I came to understand that I was afflicted with what are beautifully referred to as "night terrors."

There are conflicting ideas about whether night terrors are part of the mental health kingdom. Some say they're caused by an underlying sleep apnea condition. I had already been tested for that, and the tests had come back negative. Other experts believe that post-traumatic stress disorder has a correlation to night terrors. Despite what anyone believed or diagnosed, mine had gotten worse, becoming more frequent with each passing year. That was certainly not helping my relationships or my health. The feeling of being able to sleep, and sleep well, is something I've always craved. But a good night's sleep, which in my case means an uneventful one, was becoming increasingly elusive.

I found a counsellor. She knew about the panic attacks, the night terrors, my actual physical injuries—the whole damn mess.

"Mandy," she told me, "your receptors are on overload. People who think the way you do never admit they're broken."

"Fair enough," I said. If there's one thing I know about myself, it's that I'm always receptive enough to listen when someone is trying to educate me on something I might not know. And I knew she was on to something. We talked a bit more, and I thought I was doing okay with the conversation, but she stopped me mid-sentence and told me I was overthinking my answers.

"Just tell me a little bit about your life."

So I did. As I shared with her, I could see the tears starting to form in the corners of her eyes. I'll never forget what she said next.

"People like you, Mandy, will change the face of the earth, but it may change you before you get the chance to finish what you feel you need to do, unless you figure out how to deal with these emotions."

She told me she'd sat with me long enough to know I had "gifts and ingenious talents that are rare in our human race," as she put it. "But the truth is, brilliant or not, you have inflicted enough pain on your body, and it's inflicted enough pain back on you, that all of what you're going through will only become more acute until you make yourself a priority, and put boundaries up, and let certain people in your life walk on their own two feet."

I learned from her that a very small part of the population is like me, growing up feeling like we are supposed to be the parent. It's not the fault of our parents. It's how we're made. She told me my parents didn't ask me to look after them. But because of the instinct I had from a young age to understand people, because of my strong intuition and my feelings for people, I carried that burden.

I couldn't change who I was, or how I was emotionally responding to my family's circumstances. It would be like telling someone who was born with free enterprise in their blood that they have to go work on an assembly line. It would be like dying a slow death.

We delved right back into my childhood. We talked about my

dyslexia, and how I didn't understand back then why I was the only kid being removed from my class because I needed help not spelling words backward. No one knew what dyslexia was, or how to deal with me, and that experience could well have left scars.

Life had thrown me other curve balls, too. At ten, I was touched inappropriately (that's the politest way of saying it) by a cousin on my dad's side, who was supposed to be watching my twin and me. The confusion that set in because of the experience made the special class look like Disney. I didn't tell my parents because I knew it would hurt them, and I sensed it would have started a war I wasn't equipped to deal with, given all the "ordinary" turbulence in our family life. Even as a child, I carried that feeling of responsibility. Of course, little did I realize I was carrying the burden of holding the "ugly" inside. For a time, it worked for me. Or, I thought it did.

Food was part of this picture. A huge part.

How we ate during my childhood was simple: clam chowder, fried baloney on a regular basis—that's an East Coast delicacy, folks—and Cheese Whiz on white bread for a snack. I watched my father, who to me was invincible, pack away food like he was going into hibernation. He needed it, because he worked tirelessly from before dawn until dusk. Of course, I thought I could do the same. And I'd been taught to fill up. But holy shit, throw in the female hormones and the processed food, and we definitely have a problem, Roger.

As I matured and became increasingly busy, and given nutrition was never a topic discussed in our house, processed food was a convenience that fit in with my fast-paced life. Why would I want to have something homemade if I could rip open a box and shove the contents down my throat? When I left home and started working in the city, I worked hard and ate like a lumberjack. For a long time, I lived off chocolate chip muffins and anything takeout. Junk. Carbs. Fast food. I was addicted to being full with no metabolism to counteract it.

Food was one issue. And then there was beer. There was nothing this hoppy little beverage couldn't fix for me. I turned to alcohol to numb some of what I was feeling, even though half the time I didn't even understand where those damn feelings came from.

My whole life, I've gotten away with carrying the extra weight because of my personality. Pup used to say, "Dear, there is a good 200 and a sloppy 200. You got my looks and you have an athletic build."

I'd laugh at him and say, "You mean I got your shoulders and Ma's ass!"

"You know what I mean. I think you're perfect."

But I didn't feel perfect. Sometimes, often, I did feel okay. I'd be going through life feeling just fine, things were going well, when bam—something would hit me from left field.

I was in my early thirties, and Sara and I were in San Francisco, one of my favourite cities—not only because that was where, ten years before, I'd signed my first really big contract. Also because it's stunning. The elevations, the history, the shopping, the waterfront all play a part. I'd just met again with the Gap folks. From there, I met with the Levi Strauss team, and it was back to my favourite hotel, the Fairmont, which stands on top of Nob Hill. What I love most about the Fairmont are the life-sized gingerbread houses in the lobby. And then there's the view. From nearly any room you can see Alcatraz. Very fucking cool.

Sara had joined me on the trip. She and I had been together for a couple of years, still in our honeymoon stage. We were walking near Fisherman's Wharf, relaxed and enjoying the evening. It had been a good day. I was feeling good about where the company was going. Sara was affectionate and didn't care who saw that she loved her little Bear.

We'd come out of the Ghirardelli shop, where we bought some chocolate for Christmas stocking stuffers, when this guy walked by, looked Sara up and down, and said, "Hey, you blonde fox!"

Sara squeezed my hand, sending the "just ignore this arsehole" message.

But he wasn't finished.

"It's not bad enough that it's a waste you would sleep with another woman," he said. "But at least find one that's your calibre, and where you don't fit into both sides of her pants."

He smirked and kept walking. It was so harsh, it took our breath away. We had never experienced anything like that.

Sara looked at me, and a tear came to her eye. She tried to soothe my raw feelings. "Bear, you're the cutest, most attractive person I know."

Funnily enough, I wasn't even close to my biggest size at that time. I was chubby, I wasn't obese. But with Sara standing next to me at 5'10", nicknamed Jane Fonda for a reason, the contrast was impossible to miss. I believe the guy making the comment was uncomfortable with Sara showing her love for me. But when someone says something hateful like that, it'll take the wind out of your sails, no matter how much you tell yourself it's a classic case of small-dick syndrome—no matter how self-confident you usually are.

The thing is, it wasn't just the beer, the junk food, and whether or not I exercised enough. I'm not saying my habits don't play a role in whether or not my pants fit. But the issue goes deeper than that. It's linked to my metabolism—or lack thereof.

I can't count how many times I came home, stared at Ma, and said, "Ma, I'm looking at your midsection and hoping you're gonna give birth to my metabolism sometime soon!"

"Stop that, Mandy!" she'd say, and we would laugh, but the underlying frustration at not being able to find a fix for my weight has always been there.

I was well into my life as a full-grown Bear before I understood the link between emotion and metabolism and, thus, depression and weight gain—or, for some people, weight *loss,* damn them! The fact is, going all the way back to childhood, our household environment played a part in my stature. Weight isn't wholly based on calorie intake. In a nutshell, the more yelling and turmoil I was exposed to, the thicker I got. As many doctors have told me, people underestimate what a tense or volatile environment can do to a person's body.

It wasn't that I couldn't handle the environment at home. What took the biggest toll on me was my inability to *fix* my environment by making my parents happy. My weight was the result of a vicious circle, like a merry-go-round—without the "merry"—that I couldn't get off. I had weight issues because of my home circumstances. I had depression because of my weight issues. My depression was like Krazy Glue for weight. What a screwed-up mess. I couldn't escape from any of it, but every issue centred around my not being able to make my parents happy. All I wanted was to be able to do enough for them, so they would see me and see what I was trying to do for them. Nothing is harder than watching two people you are genetically predisposed to love like hell, hurting.

My parents were beautiful people, and I somehow thought money and material things would bring them peace. Money can do that to a point, but the reality is that we have one body, one mind, one heart. If it's broken, nobody is coming around with another one. You have to figure out how to fix that shit yourself, and let it heal over. And it's taken me my whole life to realize that when you're broken, you can't completely fix yourself. Ever.

People are not prone to thinking A-type personalities, go-getters, and leaders have mental health issues to deal with. We do. My life may look pretty from the outside, but nothing has ever been easy for me. We all fight our demons daily. Every day, I have to hit the reset button. I fight my depression every day, and I fight my weight every day. They're absolutely connected. Weight is one of the most horrible lifelong burdens, and carrying excess weight fucks up a person mentally. All I've ever wanted is to get up in the morning like most other people, put on my jeans, my shirt, and my jacket, and have them fit—because I ate the same meal you did last night.

However, I've also used my weight, depression, and panic attacks as weapons because they test my resiliency and make me stronger—better able to get back up when I'm knocked down. If I can control my depression, I have more energy to focus on other things. And I'm also keenly aware that my depression is my body's barometer, letting me know where I am at.

To be in that Ronald McDonald House thirty years after delivering my 4-H speech in those awful, hated pants opened a floodgate of emotions. It was one of the most serendipitous moments of my life. I knew the project was meant to be. And now, finally, after a lifetime of struggle, I don't care about how people look at me because I'm overweight.

I'll always have fat cells. These fat cells are the gift that keeps on giving. But it's not about the number on the scale. It's about trying to find that place where you're happy in your life. I'm not sure why some people can handle more of life's heartbreaks and misfortunes than others, any more than I understand why some are *given* more. But I know I've been blessed to have weathered the storms that have come my way. I've been told I'm part of that 1 to 2 percent of the population that is so gifted in some areas, we don't realize our brains need to process at a different level. When we don't process in that different manner, panic attacks are the result. I had to learn to rewire my own brain so I could function in life.

Sara worked her ass off to help me. As a fitness expert, she taught me about exercise and how different types of physical activity bring the body into a healthier state, nearer to a kind of harmony. She taught me how to watch my heart rate, and more. Between her soft disposition and her ability to know what I needed, the regimen she planned for me worked. Before Sara came into my life, I didn't have a clue what I needed because no one had ever taken the time to show me. I spent ten years with that beautiful woman, and I will never forget how she helped me finally get healthy.

Partway healthy, that is. More than halfway because, after my injury, my body became accustomed to panic attacks. A panic attack is a physiological reaction that will never entirely disappear. But I've mostly learned to control it. It takes awareness, and it takes effort. I talk myself down. I think about my brother Chris—this poor bastard who will never drink another Keith's, never watch another football game, never see his kids grow up—and I realize that whatever it is that's working me up is not important enough for me to go there. I don't rage anymore. I resort to gratitude.

I talk myself down.

20

EVEN BARBIE AGREES: XOE CAN BE ANYTHING

Xoe came barrelling down the sidewalk toward me screaming, "Bear!"

I picked her up and swung her around. As her cute-as-heck pink tool belt got caught on mine and fell to the pavement, I saw her cheeks flush. I scooped up the tool belt, clipped it around her waist, and said, "If that little belt wasn't so excited to get started, it wouldn't have wiggled its way off!"

She stared back at me with sea-blue eyes and giggled. Relief. Then she grabbed me around the shoulders and hugged me like I was a new stuffed bear she'd just gotten from Santa. I knew at that moment that she was the right girl for this job, and that today was going to be a life changer for both of us.

Months earlier, I'd just gotten off a flight to the Big Apple, and my cell phone, playing catch-up after its airplane-mode catnap, was dinging incessantly, telling me that Taunia, my PR queen at the time, was determined to reach me.

I felt like I had a bag on every shoulder and more besides. I fumbled with the phone and called her. She asked how my trip was.

"Sweetie, you know me. I'm grateful I woke up this morning, and extra grateful I woke up remembering why New York is not my favourite city. It's big, fast, and dirty, and some of its inhabitants have an extremely exaggerated sense of themselves and their relative place in our humble existence."

Don't misunderstand me. I appreciate many elements of the city, and my New York peeps are terrific. But was I braced for such experiences as the inevitable "treat" of being taken out to the "most fabulous" trendy new restaurant, with tabletops the size of pie plates and just enough room between those plates for an ass that hasn't eaten in eighty-three days to squeeze by? And, of course, there's the server acting like he's doing me a favour by stopping by the table thirty minutes too late (given I needed a drink upon entry) to deliver his best "Wha'd'yahavin?"

Taunia laughed. "Why can't I have more clients like you? And out of curiosity, what *is* your favourite US city?"

"Chicago."

Zero hesitation. I got excited telling Taunia how fantastic Chicago is. Food, architecture, blues, jazz, people who are proud that their city is infectious and welcoming. "And, of course, I might just be a Chicago Bears fan."

We laughed together. Then Taunia brought me up to speed on a few housekeeping items and homed in on the real reason for her calls.

But it was the wrong time for this conversation. Anyone who has ever travelled through a busy airport has felt the pain of trying to get from the gate to land transport. I had my carry-on in tow, my computer bag slung over a shoulder. I was wrestling with a set of earbuds. I was trying to keep up with what Taunia was saying: something about—was I hearing her right? Barbie? It was everything I could do not to throttle the ignorant asshole who had just cut off an older couple right in front of my eyes. And I had walked nose-first into a stink storm deposited by a confused idiot who mistakenly thought he could digest dairy.

"Can this wait?" I asked her.

Apparently it couldn't, because she blurted out, "How would you feel about a partnership with Barbie?"

A partnership with Barbie? Me? Who was she kidding? The hot blonde bombshell might have been every other little lady's Sears Christmas Wish Book dream, but when I was a kid, I would have sooner gargled with rusty tacks than see her naked *or* clothed existence under the Rennehan Christmas tree. It didn't matter how cool the wrapping paper was.

"I need to know that you're interested, Bear, because there are tight timelines on this," she replied.

Fair enough. Okay, I told her, I'm interested. Mostly so I could get off the phone. I'd learn more later. We agreed to talk when I got back to Canada in a few days. I hopped in the cab and didn't give Barbie another thought—until Taunia reached out with a follow-up call.

She'd sent me a proposal. While she was on the line, I scrolled through the first page and instantly went into belly laugh mode. Mattel was proposing a Construction Barbie contest in partnership with Freshco, with me acting as the construction "mentor."

"Bear, you said you were interested the last time we talked!"

"Taunia, my dear, I only half-understood what you were asking. I thought we were talking about a photo op for charity, not a full-blown event!"

Taunia asked me to look deeper into the request, because she felt I'd be perfect for this opportunity. I respected her opinion, so I spent that evening reconsidering my childhood arch enemy.

At first, putting me and Barbie together seemed odd. Not just odd: insane. From body type, to hair, to clothing, and everything in between, we were polar opposites. What Barbie had represented for decades certainly wasn't me. But the You Can Be Anything campaign, which Mattel was hoping we'd sign on to, aimed to shine a light on women from diverse backgrounds who were breaking boundaries in their fields, especially fields where women are just starting to make some headway. Fields like the trades. One of its goals was to inspire the next generation of girls.

This was something I could get behind. I could definitely put my North American brand together with Barbie's global brand and come out the other end with a strong message for young women. So, despite a lifetime of carefully steering clear of Barbie and her kind, my Bear brain was already thinking about the ways we at Freshco could amplify this campaign, along with the experience that would go with it.

Given my company's headquarters is in Oakville, Ontario, just outside Toronto, Mattel had assumed the Construction Barbie contest would roll out there. No way, I told them. If I was going to be their Construction Barbie mentor, we would be bringing this phenomenal opportunity to the beautiful seaside town of Yarmouth, Nova Scotia. And I'd make sure it was an event unlike anything they'd seen or done before. "Trust me on that."

Freshco and Mattel set out together to find the lucky girl who would work beside me for a one-day hands-on building experience. Parents from across Canada could enter their girls in the contest. The forms included regular information such as name and age, but the big questions they had to answer were "Why should your daughter be selected?" and "How do you feel this will change her life?"

The winner would be seen by other young girls throughout Canada and the United States. She'd get lots of prizes for working hard all day in the shop, talking to media, and being an inspiration to all the other young girls who would be looking on (with perhaps just a bit of harmless jealousy).

Because Construction Barbie was a different take on the Mattel icon from what young girls were used to—and maybe a harder sell—I rounded up my A-list Bear Squad to pull off the very best "everyone-in-pink" event (me included and happy about it, I swear!).

November in Nova Scotia can be a bit nippy, and to help ward off a bit of that chill, my team ordered cozy Barbie-pink hoodies with white graphics for me, my mentoree, the camera crews, and the terrific women in my life who would be onsite: Kat (nicknamed BSE), our strategist; Taunia (Polish, because her work was so pristine) with PR; and Nikki (Swan), our everything-fun-in-events person. We brought in white hoodies with pink graphics for the rest of the team. We took my Chevy Tahoe to a local shop and had it wrapped in pink. Yes, more pink, and I was doing surprisingly well with it. The vehicle looked exactly like a giant Barbie mobile: cool, inspiring, and hideous at the same time. Meanwhile, Freshco's brand ambassador, Jason (a.k.a. Jayfer), ordered 300 large and extra-large "You Can Be Anything Barbie" T-shirts for all the girls who turned up for the event to put over their winter coats, as the end-of-day party was scheduled to take place outside the local mall.

My girl for the day, Xoe, had been chosen from a list of twelve hundred applicants. When I found out who she was, I immediately called the head of Mattel in Toronto and said, "What are you doing to me?" Xoe was from, of all the possible places, Yarmouth—my hometown. I couldn't believe it. The choice smacked of favouritism. But I was quickly and firmly told, "Absolutely not! Xoe's story was so compelling it wouldn't have mattered where she was from." I can't tell you Xoe's story—it's not mine to tell—but as soon as I heard it, I realized they were right. There couldn't have been a more appropriate kid for this "job."

I was both relieved and excited.

The morning of the big day, Mattel's camera crew set up the introduction sequence outside my local shop. When Xoe ran out screaming my name, and we hugged, it was right out of a Hollywood tear-jerker. I nicknamed her right away: Bear Jr. We painted her new name on her pink hard hat so everyone would know that Bear and Bear Jr. were a team.

Then we got to work.

Xoe tackled everything with purpose. She painted, hammered, screwed doors on a cabinet, and even challenged me to a fun who-can-drive-the-nail-in-the-board-fastest competition. We showed her our fabulous shop and the dazzling, robotic carving capabilities of the CNC machine. Then it was time to talk with the media outlets that had been taping us. They knew a good story when they saw it. And Xoe's excitement was infectious.

I started the interviews in my usual upbeat, playful fashion. Out of the corner of my eye, I could see Bear Jr. staring at me, a little bit in awe. She knew her turn was coming up. When the reporter turned to her with some questions, she hid behind her mother and me. It was to be expected. I bent down and whispered to her, "Xoe, this is your chance to help other girls see how awesome you're doing and show them that they could love the trades, too!"

That was all it took. She grabbed my hand, asked if I'd hold her new Construction Barbie, and took hold of the microphone. My insides were melting. Confidence happens in stages, and little Xoe was fast mastering her first stage, right in front of the cameras, with a big, enthusiastic smile. I beamed with pride. At one point, a little later on, she shouted, "Everyone ready to roll?" All heads turned in her direction. Xoe had "arrived."

The entire day was less about a young girl using a hammer and nails, and more about the bigger picture around the messaging that *You Can Be Anything.* I'm a huge believer that, with the right mentorship and direction, you *can* do it all and be it all. You can be a mom, work in the trades, make lots of money—or anything else of your choosing. And our girls need to know that, like me, they can be their own boss while working in the dynamic trades industry.

It was time to head to the mall for the grand finale. The pink-wrapped Barbie mobile pulled up to the building. Pam Mood, Yarmouth's mayor, greeted us from the front seat, and we all hopped in. I'm sure Xoe thought this was a simple drive to the mall, but when she looked up and saw our escorts, her eyes grew round as saucers. We had pulled out all the stops, and some local heavy equipment operators formed a parade of trucks and backhoes, horns blowing, everyone cheering as we made our way along Yarmouth's main drag.

When we pulled into the mall parking lot, the crowd went nuts. Imagine being a young girl and seeing a full-sized Barbie truck. The noise those kids made was proof positive that we'd done this right.

We'd planned for an outdoor event, but there was lots of wind and it was calling for rain, so the mall manager insisted we take the show inside. We made our way through the crowd and into the mall. It was jam packed: three hundred little munchkins, girls and boys, wearing pink T-shirts that hit the floor, were screaming like it was a rock concert.

The crowd had been there for a while, getting their T-shirts and taking part in activities. Mattel had given out three hundred Barbies, and staff in the mall were sporting You Can Be Anything Barbie T-shirts in solidarity. Everyone was involved. The excitement and community pride in the air was infectious.

When it was time to quiet the crowd down, I told them, "I want people to love who they want, be what they want, and live the life that a lot of people before us couldn't live." They listened intently. What I was saying was encouragement for the kids, but, at the same time, it was a heads-up for the parents: Stop telling your girls what they should be doing with their lives. Stop putting them in preconceived boxes. Let them choose.

Xoe was next. Her shyness vanquished, she took the stage boldly, both hands gripping the microphone, her Barbie tucked safely in the hammer loop of her tool belt. Then she told the crowd about her great day. She said that all girls could feel the way she did, and that they can be anything they want, just like she was doing.

In the midst of Bear Jr.'s motivational words, my mother's hand reached up and rested on my shoulder. Ma, in her pink Barbie toque, kissed me on my cheek and said, "Are you sure you came out of me? Because by the looks of things, it's not only me that thinks you are incredible."

What more did I need to celebrate the dramatic pivot my girl Barbie and I had made that day as the world's oddest couple? At that point it was a toss-up between Xoe, Ma, and a cold beer. In a world where we are fighting for diversity, not everyone can be a short, cute, little bear. Some have to be tall blondes. Barbie and I are both okay with who we are. And that's the message to young girls and young women out there. Be okay with who you are, and that includes everything from wearing the clothing you feel best in, to saying "no" when someone else tries to choose your vocation for you.

For me, the true test of the day came when Xoe told me what she wanted to be when she grows up. "I want to be a construction worker," she said, with her newfound confidence. "And a karate instructor, too, because I already have an orange belt with a full black stripe. I can do both."

Yes, Xoe. You sure can.

21

—

BEWARE OF SHARKS AND OTHER HAZARDS

I was still in the early days of expanding my business beyond Canada's East Coast. Freshco had landed a job for a retailer in Montreal, a floor replacement and light renovation. A guy walked in, complete with sidekicks, and started talking to me in French. I said, "I don't speak French."

He said, "That's the issue. We don't want you here. You haven't asked to be here."

I told him this company hired me, and I'd hired local people to do the work.

"But you're from Ontario."

"From what I understand, that's not against the law."

And he said, "It's against my law. I do all the business on the street. This is what I want. If you don't find me ten grand by tomorrow, you and your client are going to have bigger issues, because I will burn this store down."

Then he walked away.

What the fuck?! I looked around me? Was this real? I couldn't believe something like this could happen outside of a bad B movie. I was blown away. I looked at one of my guys and asked, "What do I do?"

"What *do* you do?" was his only response.

Not so helpful for a Bear in a panic.

I told myself to calm the fuck down. When in trouble, call a friend. I rang a buddy back home.

"Oh my God, Bear!" she exclaimed. "I don't know what to tell you. You can't have this happen!"

No shit. But how was I supposed to stop it? "What do I do? Go to the cops?"

"But who knows what he'll do. And how are the cops going to find him? The retailer will find out, and they'll have to let you go. Then your name is mud."

She was right. And I was frightened to death. I didn't know what else to do. I drove the six hours back to Toronto that night and went to my bank first thing in the morning. I had a line of credit, and I did have the right to withdraw against it. But I remember hesitating to request ten thousand dollars in cash, for fear of the bank asking what it was for. The asshole threatening me didn't scare me, but my client finding out and the possibly of my losing the job, or any credibility, did. My reputation was all I had.

I finally took a deep breath and went in to undertake the transaction. I had no choice. And, thankfully, all went smoothly.

At three in the morning, I handed over the money. Ten thousand dollars. He had found out about me and the job I was doing through one of the guys I'd hired locally. My hard-earned cash was in his filthy hands. He said, "You know what? You did the right thing. Because not only would I burn the building, I would follow you. Because you're not French. You shouldn't be here."

In the meantime, I had my retail clients begging me, "Please help me in Quebec, please help me in Quebec!" It was no damned wonder they needed help, if this was how their contractors were treated. Extortion? Really?

Stories like this one explain why, in part, the trades have had such a horrible reputation. I was dealing with the bowels of the industry back then. I was concerned with being able to find enough honest people to help me get the job done. I sometimes wondered whether I was the only honest person I knew. I honed my how-to-read-someone skills because I needed to be surrounded by people I could trust.

Quebec wasn't the only place where I faced extortion. It happened when I first started to make inroads into the United States as well. "You shouldn't be here," was something I heard often. I didn't let it deter me, but my head was on a swivel. I was constantly watching my back.

A couple of decades and skyrocketing business growth later, I could still use advice on "scaling." But of a different kind than I thought I needed then.

In 2019 alone, Freshco turned down ten million dollars' worth of work because the company faces a systemic shortage of skilled tradespeople. I've thankfully uncovered the powerhouse of talent in women who haven't been given the opportunity to demonstrate their abilities in the construction sector. But we have to do a lot more to convince others to consider a career in this industry. Otherwise, we all lose.

The desperate shortage of skilled tradespeople in our industry is not just a challenge for my business. It's also a scary dilemma the world finds itself in. As the Blue Collar CEO, I'm doing my damnedest to draw attention to it and to turn it around. But this fight will take time.

Meanwhile, we face the stark consequences of that shortage every day.

There's also the challenge of just getting people to work, period.

I planted my butt into a cozy seat at my favourite spot in Naples, Florida. It's a beautiful restaurant and bar overlooking the waterside shops. Affluent, casual. The people-watching is sensational. My attention was drawn to a group of men sitting together in the corner. Retired and clearly set, financially.

Annie asked, "Bear? Why do you keep looking at those guys?"

"Because," I told her, "these guys were probably given or built a company in a time when people were different. When running a business was different." She knew what I meant. So many things are right today that were not right back then. But try finding people today who are committed, who will commit to you, and who have a work ethic? It's excruciating.

One of them got up and, as he walked by our table, asked, "Do I know you?"

I laughed. "Do you want to know what we're talking about?"

He joined us. Before his retirement, we learned, he'd been in fabrication and metalwork. His sons had since taken over his business. He'd started the company in the 1950s, so I asked what it was like building a business back then: mid-century, postwar. He said it wasn't easy, but he'd done well.

I was pretty sure he hadn't faced the same labour shortage we're struggling with these days. I asked him, "How did it feel to have people beg you for a job and come to work for you, grateful for a pay-cheque because of your ambition and your ability to provide them with work?"

"You know," he replied, "I never in a million years would have expected a question like that, especially from a Canadian."

About a year ago, he said, his son told him they were having prob-lems with human resources. People weren't showing up to work, many were out on stress leave . . . the list was endless. Both his sons were losing sleep, trying to figure out where they were going to get the people they needed to fill their orders.

He told them it was just a part of doing business.

Now this was a conversation we could have! I am a person who believes strongly in diversity and inclusion, and in putting pride back into an industry that is sadly lacking it. But more than ever, I find myself dealing with staff struggling with a host of difficulties. My employ-ees were coming to me, especially the younger ones with school debt hanging heavily around their necks, unable to live the lives they've been dreaming of. In turn, depression and mental health issues were on a steep rise, and we had to figure out how we could best provide support. What weighs on staff, weighs on me, because I want the very best for my employees. They're family. I want them to see the light at the end of the dark debt road. For a country that is desperately in need of tradespeople, it sure does cost a lot to become a tradesperson.

I'm also dealing with what looks, from where I sit, like an era of entitlement. Is this because of a generation of helicopter parents who, instead of teaching their children resilience and independence, have crippled their ability to think for themselves or to work for what they want? That's for psychologists and sociologists to sort out. What I know is that it doesn't bode well for my industry, where the supply-and-demand issue is killing us slowly.

I shared my thoughts with this gentleman.

"I'm going to pick up your bill today, Canada," he told me.

"It's a good fucking thing," I said, laughing. "Because the exchange rate is crap right now. You'd almost think I came down here crying poor because I couldn't pay my bill."

"No, Mandy, you made me realize that I ignored my son when he came to me, telling me the difficulties they were having at the factory. I had no idea what he was really going through, because I never had to worry about finding people. I paid them right, and they showed up every day and they never left until the job was done. Even though I'm seventy-six years old, sometimes I want to jump back in with my sons, because I can see they're struggling."

My new friend paid the bill and left Annie and me to continue the conversation. "Bear," Annie said, her voice hushed, "I've heard you talk about these things before, but I can see now that it's really bothering you."

She was right. But issues with employees were only part of what was weighing on me. I told her that people out there don't understand what pressure it is to be an entrepreneur.

Lately I'd had to deal with the realities of the economic headwinds from the United States, as major retailers restructure their facilities departments and downsize their footprints. Meanwhile, if it isn't bad enough that I'm struggling to hire enough skilled people, and then somehow keep them happy and healthy and actively *on the job*, I need to keep a high level of technological and digital expertise in-house as well, to protect my intellectual property—otherwise, anyone could come in and drown me behind my back in the middle of the night. Nobody told me I would need a police department in my office. But apparently I do.

This is one of those challenges that you learn about only once you're already knee deep in the problem. I'm no stranger to them.

They're legion. Sometimes no amount of business savvy or forecasting can predict the rough waters you'll find yourself navigating.

In the spring of 2010, Freshco was fifteen years old and on the verge of expansion into the United States, when things started to go sideways. Out of nowhere, I started receiving letters—an awful lot of letters—from lawyers. The letters said their clients were suing me.

The complaints ranged from shopping carts in ditches to tainted produce. Phone calls and emails with messages that had zero to do with my business were constant. Resumés for jobs I hadn't posted were piling up. I felt like I was in a shaken-up snow globe. Had everyone gone mad?

A little bit of digging revealed the answer, but it was an answer that only added more confusion. Sobeys, a grocery store chain that has its head office in Stellarton, Nova Scotia, was, like my company, successfully building a presence beyond the Maritimes: a good-news East Coast business story. Except that Sobeys had decided to rename its Ontario deep-discount stores FreshCo. They'd used my font. They'd even used my company colours. It was no wonder I was being inundated with their shit—nobody knew the difference between FreshCo and Freshco.

I headed straight for my lawyer, in full grizzly mode. Freshco had been launched years before Sobeys came up with FreshCo. Surely that had to count for something.

Nope.

"Welcome to Ontario," my lawyer said, who then told me that any business can incorporate under the same name as another one, as long as it's providing a different service. She further explained that because Freshco with the small "c" was only federally incorporated across Canada, and not trademarked, I didn't have a leg to stand on.

You have got to be kidding me. They could take my name because they were selling groceries and not doing retail maintenance? The sheer stupidity of such laws was mind-boggling.

I was also devastated, and worried about the fate of my company. We'd been getting a lot of traction, and I didn't want to lose ground. My first thought was to change our name, but my management team and I agreed that would not be the best idea, because our clientele knew us as Freshco. We were too far in for a name change. Plus, I thought, "I was here first, you ignorant pieces of shit!"

I even wondered, "What if they'd known I was a self-made original from the East Coast, just like them? Would it have mattered?" To this day, I still struggle with similar questions. East Coasters don't screw anyone, much less each other. I couldn't wrap my head around this one.

Over several years, I spent thousands of dollars in time and legal fees sending letters to legal counsel all over Ontario, telling them we are not the grocery store and that their clients didn't slip in our parking lot or in our aisle. That another company's irresponsible and selfish decision would cost me that much money and time was beyond frustrating.

Because the situation was so ridiculously wrong, and because I'm a problem solver who can't wallow in the "poor me" realm for very long, I decided to approach the problem with a creative solution that had a comedic flare, Mandy-style. When all else fails, laugh.

By then, five years had passed. Part of Freshco's saving grace is that the majority of our customers are Fortune 500 companies from the United States: they know nothing about FreshCo the grocery chain. For our Canadian friends and newer clients, there was a simple yet effective way to tell them we were not the grocery store. So simple, in fact, it was laugh-worthy. I teamed up with Ray Creative Agency out of Newfoundland and Labrador, and launched a national campaign in July 2015 called "Freshco (not the grocery store!)" (including the exclamation mark).

Refreshing the brand included a new website, animated videos, billboards, and new signage on our commercial vehicles. We also created a new logo in navy blue and white, with the "F" made up of a hammer and nail, so it could easily be distinguished by consumers. My site crews also got a makeover—new Freshco-branded overalls, jackets, hats, and "Safety Is Sexy" T-shirts.

The rebranding cost us a small fortune, but if there is one thing that sets Freshco (not the grocery store!) apart, it's our personality— in every aspect of our business. It was a game changer.

One small move on my company's part back in its early days would have saved us all this aggravation. Back then, in the world of .com, Canada was screaming, "We're somebody, too!" Hence, .ca was born. Sobeys launched as FreshCo.com, and we didn't realize just how big a giant .com was until we were forced to compete with it. Had I snagged both .com and .ca from the get-go, the name FreshCo would not have worked for Sobeys.

Instead, when we built our new website, we had to put a box on the front page that read, "If you are trying to get a job at the food mart called FreshCo, hit this tab," and a link would take them to the Sobeys website. That's how bad it got. And still, they emailed, called, and sent us their resumés.

I have to work at educating people every day on which company is which. And I *still* find myself sitting in meetings to which I've been invited as "Freshco's Mandy Rennehan," where people tell me how impressed they are with all I know about food distribution. I never know whether to slap them into reality in public or in private. Who invites someone to an event without even doing enough homework to know who they are? Lazy, ignorant, stunned people, that's who.

Stop it, people. Stop it!

I was in Washington, DC, a couple years ago sitting on a Canadian-American Business Council panel. There were some heavy hitters at the table, including top brass from CN, Mastercard, and Seaman. Part of the discussion focused on me as the Blue Collar CEO, trade deals and labour policies, and how none of our companies will scale properly without the right people.

Afterward, I was approached by a top executive from a beverage company who had listened to the panel discussion. Or, I thought she had.

"Oh my God, Mandy," she said, "what you said was wonderful. I love the Blue Collar CEO, and I just wanted to thank you so much for your support in carrying our products in your stores."

What part of "Freshco (not the grocery store!)" had she not heard me discussing? And how can multi-billion-dollar companies grow with people like her working for them?

I gave a shake of my head and carried on. There are times when that's all you can do, and that's all that's required. There are times when it equates to real victory. Carry on. Keep doing what you do best.

22

GO HOME, RESTORE THE WINDMILL, AND THEN SOME

They say the sea calls you back home. Twenty years after I'd left Yarmouth, my soul was yearning for the place that had raised me: my family, the food, our rich history and architecture. Sara and I packed up the truck with suitcases and our two basset hounds, Maggie and Doug, and headed east. The plan was to stay a full month, longer if we could swing it.

After many long hours on the road from southern Ontario through Quebec and New Brunswick, we finally arrived. We turned up the driveway of the Rennehan compound: a breathtaking 18-acre historic windmill property on the hill of Old Post Road, overlooking a pristine lake and, beyond that, the Atlantic Ocean. I'd bought the property eight years before and had been restoring it, piece by piece. My whole body immediately relaxed. We stopped the car and let the dogs out. They ran through the fields, no leads attached and nobody calling them back.

The windmill stared back at me like I was her long-lost love. I unlocked her front door and stepped inside to the potent smell of dampness and bird droppings. I rubbed her bones and, at that moment, made a commitment to myself: to bring her back to her former glory, and beyond.

I had been home for less than forty-five minutes, and my heart was happy.

The Cape Cod beauty at the front of the property stood proudly beside the horse stable, its workshop, and the carriage house. Walking toward the house, I could see Pup standing on the steps, grin as wide as his face, happy to see us. He saw that I'd been in the windmill, and his first words were, "We should knock down that old thing and put a new cottage there for you and Sara."

"That would be where you are mistaken, my huge pain in the ass," I said. "She'll be a cottage all right, but her original structure will be her backbone."

"Dear, now why would you do that? Look at the condition it's in, and the bird shit it's covered in. It seems like a waste of time and money to me."

I grabbed him by the neck and threw him into a headlock, both of us laughing.

"Do I question you about your deer stands in hunting season, you nincompoop?" I let him go and tried to get serious. "Pup, you know I believe in respecting the heartbeat of history. We need to write a new chapter for her, and you're going to love it!"

Pup grinned at me. "Well, dear, it's your money. But I would take it down."

This back-and-forth banter, this refusal to see eye to eye, was part of coming home, familiar and comforting in its way. And, as I often did when Pup and I disagreed, I changed the subject.

"Okay, where are the lobsters? Or do I need a new host?"

"Look in the fridge, smart ass."

We went inside the house, opened the refrigerator, and there they were: those beautiful red crustaceans sitting in a huge bowl, like popcorn with claws, ready for a party on the hill. All we were missing was a cold beer and a card game, which we quickly arranged.

I didn't know it yet, but I was about to get up close and personal with the "heartbeat of history" that throbbed not just in the windmill itself, but also throughout my struggling hometown. In hindsight, I could look back on that windmill acreage as my gateway drug to a vast local restoration and commercial rejuvenation project.

Otherwise known as my Yarmouth property-buying spree.

As a girl riding the bus to school, I would pass by the windmill property every day, my forehead flattened against the window as I stared at that weathered, majestic old building with its giant rotating blades. I wondered at its inner workings. Sometimes a group of us kids snuck right into the building and tiptoed up the stairs. I dreamed of someday living inside it. It worked on me like some form of magic.

One of my friends back then was a girl named Red. She was determined to be a hairstylist, and I was her guinea pig for practising perms. As payback for making me look more eighties and feminine than I was comfortable with, I'd kick her ass in badminton. She was certainly my first crush.

While I moved away, found my inner lesbian, and built my business, Red had stayed in the community, married, had two kids, and built her own business as a stylist. She lived in the Cape Cod farmhouse that stood at the entrance of the windmill property. We'd lost touch, and when the property came up for sale in 2004, I had no idea who lived there, let alone that the owner was an old friend.

Living in Toronto, I was used to a half-a-million-dollar price tag for real estate the size of a postage stamp, so property prices in my hometown in rural Nova Scotia felt like giveaways. When I saw that the vast property I'd dreamed of owning since childhood listed for just $240,000, I knew this was my chance. Then, when I saw Red's name on the paperwork, I smiled. I didn't hesitate: I immediately offered her asking price, with no conditions. This was Yarmouth in 2004, and trust me when I say that no one ever offered asking price, much less without conditions.

I waited, smile still on my face and butterflies in my stomach, for the real estate agent to tell me Red's response. Given my offer, I shouldn't have been nervous, but that property meant so much to me, I couldn't help it. It didn't take long. I was told that when Red saw that the offer was from me, her face lit up. We signed the documents and sealed the deal together by popping open a bottle of vintage wine.

It was great to reconnect, especially under these circumstances, which suited us both so well. I learned that Red and her husband had divorced, and she'd found herself saddled with this massive property that she couldn't maintain. Indeed, aside from the main house, they'd done little to keep the place up. The fields were overgrown. The windmill had been built in the 1950s and, like the mansion itself, looked overgrown and dilapidated. The horse barn, which her husband had used for storing his fishing equipment and keeping some chickens, was rat infested.

I didn't care. By that point in my career, I could afford Red's price plus what was required to bring the property back to life.

—

In the early 1800s, our property, once known as Windmill Farms, was part of the estate belonging to the Churchill family, whose mansion still sits directly across the road. When the two properties were still one, our portion was the servants' quarters. The farm fields and flawlessly built stone walls that still stand on both sides of the street are a testament to the consummate integrity of the craft in that era.

Aaron Flint Churchill, the mansion's namesake, was born in Yarmouth and became one of North America's biggest shipbuilding magnates. He was well known for his massive donations to support the rebuilding of Halifax after the deadly 1917 explosion that levelled more than half of Nova Scotia's capital city and claimed about two thousand lives.

My grade six class visited the mansion. It absolutely looked and felt haunted, especially to an eleven-year-old. The caretaker (who seemed spooky to us) showed us a dungeon in the basement. Beside it was a passage to the underground tunnel that led to the property across the street. When I bought that place many years later, I went into the basement to try to find any trace of an entrance to that underground tunnel. I saw nothing to indicate it had ever existed, but I know it was there at one time.

I turned my attention to the work that was desperately needed to bring the property back to its former glory and to what is now an architectural gem that's been featured in magazines throughout North America. This project began with hoisting that rat-infested barn onto the back of a truck and delivering it to the neighbour down the road.

God, I love home improvement.

My parents divorced several years after I'd bought Windmill Farms (now known locally as the Rennehan compound) and not long after my brother Chris died. At first, they each wanted the farmhouse, which not only has the same spectacular views as the windmill but also holds all their last memories of Chris. Since the house and the property would take a great deal of upkeep, we decided it was best for Pup to stay. But Ma didn't want to be far away, especially given her newfound pastime of mowing the property.

Ma asked that we find something big enough for both her and Pigeon (that's my brother Troy), who was sober and doing better than he had in years. He was making up for lost time by spoiling her with his superb cooking skills, and it was great to have his son Cody around, too. A house that sat inches from the sand dunes in Port Maitland, a five-minute drive down the road from Windmill Farms— and, incidentally, my favourite local beach—had been put up for sale that year by an American family. Given its rough condition, the price tag was more than it was worth, but a weak real estate market meant I could bid low: I was able to secure it for $190,000.

The view from the massive front windows is arrestingly beautiful, especially with the evening sunsets, no two alike, falling over the western skies. Because of its right-on-the-beach location, the property is also privy to dramatic exhibitions of the tides the Bay of Fundy is so famous for, the sound of waves crashing against the sand, and a nearby wharf that is home to a group of local lobster fishermen who steam in and out of the breakwater. What both the beach house and the windmill have in common is the energy of my family—and our gratitude that we own these properties.

Possibly my improvement kick had rubbed off on Ma. Owning and fixing up these properties, combined with her newfound independence, inspired a sense of possibility in her. Or maybe just her fight.

Yarmouth was in rough shape. I'd known this, of course—but it was devastating to realize, on this latest visit home, the depth of the town's economic downturn. Ma had never been outwardly opinionated on matters or people, but lately she'd openly share her excitement about some female advancement in the community, and her new favourite person was Pam Mood, Yarmouth's recently elected mayor.

"Pam is awesome," she told me on a number of occasions, in her best "You'd better be hearing what I'm telling you" voice. "It's so nice to feel the energy she brings to Yarmouth, unlike the typical old men we're used to."

When Ma shared, she was blunt. When it became clear she was hoping I'd connect with Pam, I knew what I had to do.

Our bond had strengthened in the years since I'd left home, when I was seventeen. I'd told Ma at the time that I was gay. After she finished crying—it took a while—she explained that the tears were not over the fact that I was gay, but because she was afraid of how Pup would react. Ma told me she really didn't understand how one woman could be in love with another woman. But she asked, "Does it really matter?" That conversation, twenty-eight years ago, was quite different from one you might expect today, but Ma understood the most important thing—that she didn't *have* to understand—and that was huge. She said it in her own beautiful, kind, honest way.

What did anybody know about being gay back then? It wasn't necessarily general knowledge that this was a natural occurrence, that it couldn't be caused by someone or something—an event in a person's life. At one point in our conversation, Ma said, through tears, "Mandy, I feel part of this is my fault."

"Ma, why would you ever think that?"

I could feel the tears welling up in my own eyes, because she'd never spoken to me like that before, so openly, so unsure.

"Mandy, all those times you tried to get my attention, all the times you ached for my love and I didn't give it to you."

I stared at her, snotty nose and all, and asked, "Why didn't you, Ma?"

"Because I was jealous of you."

Holy shit, I could feel my insides churning. But I also felt a tightness around my heart ease. What Ma was saying made sense—in an insane kind of way.

"You were always the bright light in your father's eyes, from the moment you were born. And as you grew up, his affections for you were very evident, and as awful and sick as this sounds, I felt you were getting enough attention and didn't need my time. Please, forgive me, Mandy. Please."

I'll never forget the relief I felt at that moment. This was Ma, telling me how she really felt. What we were discussing had weighed on her for years. For me, it was the answer to the question I'd always carried with me: whether I was worthy of her love.

Today, Ma is well aware that she had no effect on my being gay. But that day, in admitting to me how she'd treated me growing up, Ma told me the truth. She was so unhappy and alone, with not a shred of self-worth, that she took it out on me because I seemed to know how to make people happy, especially my father.

I hugged her for what seemed like an eternity and let her know how much I admired her for sharing something that set us both free to love each other on a whole different level for the rest of our lives.

I was as worried about Yarmouth as Ma was. But I was also just happy to do something that I knew would please her. I called Mayor Mood.

"Hello, thank you for calling the Town of Yarmouth. How may I direct your call?"

"I am looking for Pam Mood, please," I said politely.

I was sure she was thinking, "You and hundreds more." But she said, "I will see if the mayor is in. May I tell her who is calling?"

A moment later Pam Mood was on the line, exclaiming, "Mandy Rennehan! How the heck are you? And to what do I owe this pleasure? Pam Mood at your service."

I knew right then that this woman and I would become great friends. I told her my ma had all but ordered me to get in touch with her.

"I love your mother," she said. "We've been going to the same church for years, and she's in my bible study. Every time the church needs something, big or little, she tells us she's going to call Mandy!"

We both got a chuckle out of that.

"I can't say no to Ma," I told the mayor. "She's a woman of very few words, except when she's blackmailing me with love over something she thinks she needs, or when she knows someone else is in need and I can help. But I'll tell you, Ma is a huge fan of yours, and, given the vote count in the election, I would say the vast majority of Yarmouthians are fans as well."

We got down to business: the desperate state of the town. She told me how gut-wrenching it had been when the provincial government changed hands; under the NDP the local ferry service to and from Maine, which had fed the region's tourism industry for more than a century, was cancelled. On top of that, passenger service from the Yarmouth International Airport had ceased, and there had been no out-of-city train or bus for over a decade.

"I'll dig us out of this mess," she told me, with fierce determination, "but it won't be overnight."

"Can you use some help, Mayor?"

There was a short silence.

"Mandy, I know enough about you to know you will follow through on the offer. So, yes. Absolutely. Let's do this."

Pam took time out of her busy schedule to reacquaint me with the downtown core. With that very first phone call we'd felt like friends. In person, as we discussed the massive undertaking of turning a town around, we quickly became family.

Sara, born and bred in Ontario, was blown away by the architecture and price tags on downtown Yarmouth's majestic properties, which she referred to as "giving them away." She couldn't believe what she was seeing.

"Holy shit, Bear. You couldn't buy a shed in the city for these prices."

I was absolutely in my glory, in the heavenly "restoring" sandbox of my mind. Here, I knew I could use all my design thoughts and building gifts, and turn them into Mandy masterpieces that only a historic seafaring community like Yarmouth could wear.

Even though properties were selling at a fraction of the price of those in Central and Western Canada, I would need to select and purchase strategically, as material and shipping costs were higher, given our location. Labour costs were not much cheaper than elsewhere, and it was important for me to hire as much local talent as possible.

Within my first two weeks at home, I'd bought the old town jail that stood proudly, although a bit forlorn and in need of attention, on Main Street. An American couple, feeling the effects of the loss of the ferry, had decided to abandon their own plans for the property and return to the United States. But seriously, who buys a jail? Me, apparently. This piece of brick-and-granite nineteenth-century architecture was riddled with stories and begging to be loved. I recalled how often we'd walk by this spooky masterpiece during our school lunch hours. The property was surrounded by a brutally ugly fence, topped with barbed wire, that had been added in the 1960s. That was the first thing to go, and the building stood even taller and prouder.

Thoughts of what this building could be consumed my mind. Boutique hotel? Steak and seafood house with a brew pub, perhaps? The branding opportunities were off the charts, especially given it was the oldest original jailhouse in Nova Scotia. Check!

My next purchase was a piece of land in the middle of town that overlooks the harbour. I quickly had the uninhabitable house on the property, an eyesore, demolished, loaded into a dump truck, and sent off to the landfill. The site had been for sale for some time, and I couldn't figure out why nobody had scooped it up. It did back on to two commercial parking lots—not exactly desirable, except to a visionary Bear.

The next property I found blew me away. On a quaint side street in the historic district bordering the downtown core stood a stunning old sea captain's home that predated the local neoclassical architecture. It had a bit of Gothic revival with Italianate Villa styling. To say it needed a full restoration inside and out would be an understatement, but I could see its hidden beauty. It took only pennies to purchase her, she was in that bad shape.

Over the next few years, I began work on bringing these properties up to their potential. We put a tasteful addition on the old sea captain's home, modernized the footprint with contemporary amenities, and moulded her into a gorgeous specimen. On the downtown property with the harbour view, the plan was to excavate the side of the hill and reinforce pilings that would become the foundation for a double garage, above which we'd add two more storeys to take in a view of the working waterfront, the Bay of Fundy, and the ocean beyond. For anyone wanting terrific amenities without the hassle of a big yard, check!

My vision for these buildings wasn't always clear to the local crews I'd hired. They'd shake their heads in sheer bewilderment, laughing as I told them what I wanted done. But I'd encourage them to keep going. "I promise you, you'll see what I'm seeing. And I guarantee you'll brag about your work when we're finished!"

"Okay, Renne." That's what most of them called me.

To their credit, the boys kept building off the Bear blueprints and learned a lot in the process. They were proud to call the results their own—not only were they cool projects others would never dare tackle, they were also executed with top-notch-quality work.

In the midst of purchasing and redeveloping these properties, I took a step back and visited my new friend Mayor Mood. I wanted to know what her priorities were for revitalizing the town, and how I could help push things forward. She had a ready answer. "Mandy, you look to the south end of Yarmouth, because that's where the history and heritage of our town began."

The mayor had grown up in south Yarmouth, the daughter of a local shop owner, in the days before big box stores. "The people are solid," she told me. "They would give you the shirts off their backs. They always treated our family with respect and kindness. But this end of town, for whatever ridiculous reasons, has gotten a bad rap. It pisses me off!"

I like that the mayor doesn't mince her words. She gave me a quick local history lesson. The south end, for a long time, had been the affluent area of town, which is part of the reason the period architecture there is so stunning. For too long, though, real estate agents had steered folks clear of the area—not just buyers, but developers, too. Just the thought of this caused steam to pour out the mayor's ears.

"What the level heck! If you can't sell property in a part of town where it all began, with the rich history, the sea captains' homes, the views of the ocean, all of it, then what in the name of Pete are you doing in real estate? It's disgraceful, and I'll turn it around come hell or high water."

We set out looking for a property to get started on. We saw the "For Sale" sign on the building at the same time, and smiled at each other. It was on the main corner of south Yarmouth, a place that, a little over a hundred years ago, bustled with horse-drawn carriages, merchants from all over the world, and family-owned businesses. That corner was the heart of the area.

The property we were eyeing was surrounded by others that looked as if they, too, might be for sale. Bonus. If I could purchase all four in a row, we'd have something to work with. The buildings had been home to small local shops (now closed down), a centre for people with disabilities that had just been rebuilt across the street, and a slew of drug dens. Not exactly pretty. But oh, the potential.

We weren't the only ones who saw possibility there. Myra, an old buddy from my softball-playing days, had opened Mern's Place, a popular diner, on the opposite corner. When we were kids, I was known as Young Bear, while she was Queen of the South. You've never had clams and chips and succulent coconut cream pie until you've tasted Myra's. And the great thing about her—and her having gone into business in south Yarmouth—is that she has always, in her own quiet way, made sure those in need were fed and looked after.

On our corner, we got to work creating new commercial space on the bottom, and sexy, residential apartments on the top, all with a harbour view. The original brick, which sat below layers and layers of oil-based paint, made me crazy with delight. And when all was said and done, Yarmouth had an updated version of "industrial luxury" that helped bring this corner back to life, community pride intact. I had invested over seven digits into that property, and gladly.

As I contributed in the way that I could, one restoration project at a time, Mayor Mood generated excitement and energy throughout the town. By 2016, helped along by a change in provincial government and a return of the ferry, the economic downturn had begun to shift. Homeowners and entrepreneurs took pleasure and pride in updating and improving their properties.

But my first order of business had been to finish the windmill project so I had my own place to lay my head. After cleaning out disgusting volumes of seagull shit—and keeping out the gulls with chicken wire over the windows—I approached the place with an abundance of respect for its original Douglas Fir post-and-beam construction. I found a local company to install built-in cabinetry in the kitchen and the main room. We installed garden doors out back, and put in a spa-like bathroom. We made the place cozy and snug against the ferocious winds.

Red came over one evening to check on my progress and to help me finish off a bottle of wine with a side of lobster dip.

We sat in front of my newly built, massive *Game of Thrones* fireplace, constructed with beach stones, its mantle a gorgeous piece of driftwood I'd hauled home myself from Port Maitland beach.

Red, who'd unwittingly got me started on investing in Yarmouth all those years before, when she sold me this windmill property, had by now been in business for more than a quarter-century. She owned a luxury hair boutique and spa, with an adjacent shoe and clothing shop under a separate name. But she wasn't exactly basking in Yarmouth's rising prospects. Instead, after struggling for so long through the local "depression" era, she was burnt out.

"Do you go through this, Mandy? The sheer exhaustion of owning a business and trying to make a difference?" She stared into her wine glass.

Red was one of my old friends who didn't call me by my nicknames, so she always sounded so serious.

"Every day, Red," I told her. "Even after all these years, and I can tell you many other entrepreneurs also feel like this, so you're not alone." I told her it was like shifting all the way to fifth gear, never letting up, then running out of gas in a desert.

"Yes, that's it! So, what do I do?"

"Sweetie," I told her, "you have two options. You can try to sell the business as a whole or in parts. Or, if you can't or don't want to do that, switch to a different model sedan with an automatic transmission."

She looked at me. It was as if she could hear the gears turning in my brain. "I'm listening."

Wine top-ups into both our glasses was the respectful thing to do, as we were both on the edge of our seats.

"Okay. Let's start with the fact that you're well known, and well respected, in this region. You have a following, and you are the go-to fashionista. Frankly, your style and buying abilities far exceed what I've seen even in the big cities."

I put everything I saw in front of her. She was the owner of a turn-of-the-century building in the middle of town, right off Main Street, with a harbour view. She had the potential to be the best-in-class shop in the whole province.

More wine poured. Lobster dip now nonexistent.

"I would rebrand the entire company under one name that encompasses all the services you provide. And I'd call it The Style Merchant."

Her eyes got big. She sat back and stared at me. I caught in her expression a glint of the fire that had propelled her into business twenty-five-plus years earlier. We were on to something.

I told her I knew it was a big decision. "But I will design and build it for you at cost, because this won't just benefit you—it'll benefit the entire town."

The mayor and I had chatted frequently about the need for more amenities in town to draw people here. A high-end spa would be a great start.

By the time Red left that evening, her fatigue had been replaced with excitement.

Four months later, The Style Merchant's renovation was underway, beginning with a custom 12-foot-by-64-foot mural by world-renowned local artist Brian Porter. It harkens to the Victorian and Edwardian eras, with a queen's carriage being pulled not by horses but, in true Yarmouth style, two jumbo lobsters. The queen holds the reins in one hand and wields a whip in the other. Cheeky, local, brilliant.

To celebrate the old merchant era, we found boots and shoes from the 1800s and 1900s and turned them into chandeliers for the retail portion of the shop. We were also able to build two magnificent feature walls out of bricks from the south buildings, and we added an 8-foot-tall steel cell door—sandblasted—from the jailhouse. Every detail of the project was special. I was so grateful that Red had put her faith and trust in me to do this work. She'd made the right decision: it wasn't her words that told me, or even the rising prospects for her business. It was the way she glowed every time she spoke of The Style Merchant.

The town, meanwhile, was bringing in initiatives such as a facade program (if you spent ten thousand dollars on your facade, the town would match it), a murals program, and more, to encourage home-owners and businesses to beautify properties that deserved to be loved. The mayor was full of optimism. "Mandy," she said, "these projects you're taking on are giving people hope again, and permission to make changes in their own businesses; permission to up their game. Your kind of badass is just what we've needed. Now let's celebrate by finding you another project!"

We laughed. We both knew: I was just getting started.

23

—

TRUE CAPTAINS NAVIGATE THE SWELLS

I n the fall of 2019, my partner, Annie, said, "Bear, you can't keep up this pace! You're not sleeping, and your health is suffering."

Annie was right, and while I knew she was right, my entrepreneur wiring and ambition made it hard to admit. But I did know I had to slow down, and my body was craving a climate filled with sunny vitamin D and a side order of Ma. I called her up.

"Ma, how about a six-week trip to Florida? I have a keynote in California, and then a meeting in Ottawa, and then we can meet in Florida. You game?"

"Mandy," she said, "you know your mother's rules. I'll gladly go. I want to see if you're actually going to relax. But you have to come get me."

Damn. I'd tried to sneak one by her, but I knew Ma didn't like flying alone. So I flew into Halifax to pick up my little ball of love and sarcasm, and off to southwest Florida we went, bikinis in tow.

It was March 4, 2020.

Say what you will about Florida—it's full of Q-Tips, it's God's waiting room, whatever. All I could smell was the sweet sea air, and all I could see were happy snowbirds, grateful to be there in the months before the arrival of so-called Canadian spring. Annie is a wonderful cook, and she loves experimenting in the kitchen, so Ma and I let her spoil us with culinary creations as we floated around the pool, soaking up the sunshine.

I began my days taking care of work priorities that I couldn't delegate, then spent the remainder of the time with Annie and Ma, with a tennis or golf game thrown in for good measure. It didn't take long before my stressed outer layer began to peel off.

The weekend came, and I had my paws on every newspaper southwest Florida flew in. I'm a current events, business trends, economics, and frankly anything-worth-reading junkie. I was super happy to spend my morning reading in the Sunshine State. Except that I noticed a common thread in all the papers. China + Covid virus = potential world pandemic. World leaders were meeting to discuss other countries' exposure. I lingered on a page for a while thinking surely this isn't as bad as it seems.

Didn't most people think that at first? I bookmarked it in my mind. Monday, I would make a few phone calls to see if this so-called pandemic had any legs. Meanwhile, time for a cocktail. It was afternoon somewhere in the world.

But by Monday at noon, the calls were coming in. The Canadian government started issuing alerts calling on all Canadians outside the country to return immediately. Insurance companies were saying they would cut off medical benefits if protocols weren't followed.

I started to make phone calls to friends who would know what was going on with this Covid virus.

By 6 p.m., Annie came out with a very beautiful martini and said, "I see you've been on the phone all day. I thought this would act as a relaxer."

I looked up at her. She immediately knew something was wrong. "What, Bear?"

I told her she was going to need a drink, too. I yelled to Ma to come downstairs and have dinner with us. When we were face to face, she asked outright, "What's the matter?"

"We need to leave," I told her. "Soon."

"Is it this virus thing, Mandy?"

"Yes, Ma, and we are going to drive back to Toronto, and when we get there we'll have to quarantine for a while."

"Can we go to the beach at least, before we go?"

I laughed and told her of course, that we could go before we left. She smiled. That helped. Until they closed the beaches down.

This pandemic shit was becoming very real, very fast.

I didn't want to upset Momma Bear, but I was less worried about the beaches and quarantine, and more concerned about my business. Canadian and US retailers were shutting their stores down to contain the virus. My teams on both sides of the border were disoriented and shocked. I decided to have our staff work from home. It would be a great time for the team to catch up on new training and implementations. At first, governments were talking about closing schools and urging people to stay home for a couple of weeks, to stop the virus in its tracks. But two of my highly trusted sources informed me that shutdowns and lockdowns could last for a minimum of three or four months.

I was on speed dial with my CFO, asking her for all the relevant information for me to analyze. The previous year, we had put millions into lease-hold improvements, digital expansions, staff development and training, and sales pipelines for the growth we were projecting in 2020–21. As the sole shareholder, and being self-financed, I felt like I had been placed in a war.

I knew some drastic decisions would have to be made, but for the next forty-eight hours, all I could concentrate on was getting my special ladies home: safe, reasonably happy, and stress-free.

Neither my mother nor her mother had lived through a pandemic. This was undiscovered territory. But I had been through enough in my career to understand the warning signals and what they meant. I knew this was heading toward every level of society, and we were not prepared to handle it mentally, socially, economically, or physically— and, in some respects, not even logically.

As we drove across the border, I felt some relief, but I was doing everything in my power not to show the panic that had been brewing in me for three days. I had built my company to withstand nasty weather. But a tsunami?

Only time would tell. Let the shit show begin.

Down home, as a fishing community, we used to say that anybody could call themselves a captain in calm seas, but only a true captain can navigate the swells on a stormy, unforgiving ocean. This pandemic and all she was bringing with her would call for real captains. After analyzing the tremendous headwinds in front of us, I had to make the excruciating decision to throw out a very small life raft. I would need to keep my true captains, those who could be the most flexible and agile in a storm, and leave a lot of our newer staff on the ship to wait for us to come back and get them.

I'd always believed you could see the true character of a person only when they were tested under the worst conditions. Seeing this play out in real life was another story. Fear causes the weak to do some disappointing things. There were times I was completely astonished, and frankly bewildered, by some behaviours I was seeing—outside my company and also, in a few cases, within. It appeared that I, too, had hired some "calm-seas captains." They were the ones who didn't want to put energy into what had to be done to see the business come out the other side. For these people, the crisis wasn't about binding together. It became, very selfishly, "What about me?" It was disappointing.

We had to do things quickly. Step one was to reduce our office space from eight units down to three. We closed our mill shop, which we'd opened chiefly as a convenience for our customers. It was just on its way to finally earning its keep. Closing it was one of those things that killed me, but I had to do it. As hard as it was, that retrenching became an opportunity to take stock, to see where things were happening that didn't need to be happening. We had warehouses full of stuff, much of it long forgotten, so what was it for? Why were we paying for its storage?

It was interesting, and encouraging, to see who pulled forward: those who said, "I'll take the wheel tonight. It doesn't matter about the weather." Some of them didn't even understand yet how to steer, but they were there. And I thought, *Well, if you're going to put the time into me, I'm going to put the time into you.* As the surreal months stretched on, I was able to mentor, one-on-one, several operational people in my company. They would never have seen that before the pandemic: Phone calls. Visits. Lots of aggravation, lots of anxiety, lots of "I can't do this" met with "By the love of fuck, yes you *can* do it." What I tried to instill in my team was: This pandemic will end.

But the personal growth you take from it will set you up to do anything. You can't quit. If you have to take a day off, take a deep breath, I'll cover you. *But you can't quit.* I was vulnerable with them. I might look like I'm driving through a tornado eating a donut and drinking a coffee from Starbucks, but I'm really that duck who's paddling like a mother-fucker.

I needed them to know that, just because it wasn't easy, didn't mean it wasn't possible.

Janet St Pierre Jones, a.k.a. Kitten, my senior accountant, CFO of seventeen years, and friend, was the co-captain I needed to steer the Freshco ship. And I'll be giving her Bear hugs for the rest of our lives to thank her. "Bear," she said to me at one point, "we're blowing through the retained earnings of the company, and I know you don't want to hear it, but we should apply for a loan while interest rates are low."

Nope, I didn't want to hear it, but she was right. Good call, Kitten.

After sending in all our financials and my left leg and right thumb as collateral, the underwriter came back and said, "Can you please send us real projections?"

I couldn't believe what she'd just asked. I picked up the phone and called the account manager and I said calmly but very sarcastically, "Do you want us to lie on the application?"

"Mandy, of course we don't!"

"Then what do 'real projections' look like in the eye of a fucking tornado? Have any of you ever owned a business? Employed people? Laid people off for the first time in twenty-six years? Have you ever been self-employed? This damn virus just massacred my company and people's livelihoods, I'm trying to keep people employed and save my business, and you ask stupid, patronizing questions not once, but twice, about 'real numbers'? I and millions of other entrepreneurs will not be able to check your very formulaic box this time around. So how about some goddamn respect for the information that was provided pre-Covid and pretend that maybe, just maybe, you're not doing me a favour—I am doing you one by paying you back in spades, with real interest, for your 'real' job security."

That was a mouthful, but I wasn't finished.

"This phone call is unfortunate, and also not personal, please understand. But like me, you need to pivot out of your institutional ways of thinking if you're going to call yourselves a business bank, especially in the middle of a pandemic that we've not experienced in a century. My financial history is flawless, and I will survive and thrive again, but I will not be disrespected."

I was finished with her. For the moment.

"Mandy," she said, "thank you for your candour. I will make sure that part is omitted."

"Perfect," I replied calmly, still boiling on the inside. "It was nice doing business with you."

A couple of days later, I learned that truckers and tradespeople had nowhere to go to the washroom in the midst of all the chaos. So, while all the privileged folks, including myself, could stay at home to work, we had tradespeople working around the clock for emergencies—infrastructure and maintenance projects that couldn't be put on hold. We had truckers and couriers out on the roads and highways distributing essential supplies to hospitals and grocery stores. And while most us were home uncorking that second bottle of wine, nobody had given a thought to these essential trade professionals, particularly not to where they would be able to use a washroom, wash their hands, and be safe doing so. Restaurants were closed, and drivers were turned away by businesses. There was nowhere for them to eat or grab a coffee. They could have refused to work. But they kept on, knowing how essential they were.

I've learned, over the run of my career, that when you're getting your teeth kicked in, it's not the time to stop and have a pity party. That only makes one a victim of circumstance. Instead, we have to look at the hidden, unexpected—sometimes glaringly obvious—opportunities. In this case, we at Freshco had the chance to step up for our couriers and truckers: we could use the Cadillac trailers that we had in storage to help the very people who were helping all of us. These trailers are "Cadillac" as in washroom-equipped and totally souped up. They're accessible, have running water, foot-pedal flushing, lights, air conditioning, radios, touch-free soap dispensers, and tampons. Everybody has their own stall. (We were the first company, incidentally, to put non-gendered washrooms on worksites.) These trailers check every box for what an exterior washroom can and should be.

At our headquarters in Oakville, just off the Queen Elizabeth Way, the main artery to and from the Buffalo-Niagara border, we set up four of them (with Freshco.ca (not the grocery store!) plastered on the side), completely stocked with personal protective equipment, hot water, and separate stalls. We hung two 60-foot banners that said, next to a big fucking happy face, "Truckers #Heroes," and "Clean Washrooms in Back 24/7." I live down the street from our offices, and with the rest of my staff busy pulling their weight in other areas, I stopped by daily to clean and sanitize the trailers, coming full circle to those early days I'd spent cleaning the pubs in downtown Halifax, when I was just starting out.

One half-decent day, after we'd put the trailers up, my chief operating officer and I sat in the back of one of the offices with the garage door open, watching courier after courier stop on their way to do their business. With dignity. Most of them were women, who of course have fewer options than men for comfortably peeing on the go. One of the FedEx ladies saw me. "Are you Mandy? By the love of God, I could hug the arse off you. You are the only person who would listen."

Getting notes of gratitude from these essential workers on the backs of their power bills or cable bills—as the cabs of their trucks had become their full-time offices—was a heart burster. I'm overwhelmed with thankfulness for what our blue collar workers do every day, and just as thrilled we could help in some small way.

Meanwhile, Covid shone a light for the consumer on just how bad the supply-and-demand issue really is in the trades industry. With people at home wanting to do home upgrades, lumberyards ran out of product. Who would have foreseen that happening? People in the trades were booked a year in advance and often didn't even have time to call potential clients back. It got that busy. I take no pleasure in knowing that Covid has helped people see I was right: we're in a shit-load of trouble.

Part of navigating the swells means staying true to your principles even in rough seas. Each year I give a lot of money to my various charities and other philanthropic projects. This year it was tight. Very tight. So I looked for alternative routes—a creative way to help in a real, tangible way. One day it hit me. The perfect thing. On a Zoom call with my closest colleagues and my sweet Annie, I said, "Entrepreneurs need some fun, some hope, and a challenge to keep their spirits alive. So let's buy the jailforfree.com domain!"

I watched as the four people on the screen tilted their heads in "WTF" mode, like puppies seeing you holding a shit bag but hoping it might actually be filled with organic treats. The thought needed to percolate.

"Bear, what are you smoking?" I forget who said that. But we all laughed.

"Listen," I said, "it's already paid for." The jail, I meant. The historic Yarmouth jail I'd picked up in my revitalize-my-hometown spending spree. "Nova Scotia has had huge blows to her heart and economy, and we are going to hold a massive competition across Canada and the United States and give the jail to the entrepreneur with the best idea for it and the best strategy to back that idea up."

There was silence. Then smiles and chiclets started to pop up on the screen.

"You are a crass ass, Bear, but this is going to be awesome!"

"I resemble that remark," I replied.

I gave the jail to a wonderful couple with outstanding forward-thinking plans for it: a local brewery (cleverly using the old jail in its branding) and a bistro, with a business incubator in the back. Because I obviously have a vested interest in the transformation of the jail, even though I no longer own it, I shared Mini's information with them—a.k.a. local entrepreneur Julie Mood, of Julie Mood Interiors. "I hope you will use this young woman in the trades for your project, and highlight her work," I told the new owners. I believe in Mini and in her talent. And I am 100 percent behind her philosophy of supporting other women in the trades: work and experience for Mini means work and experience for other women, following in her footsteps. Every single female hire is a step toward change.

As I write this chapter, we are what feels like a hundred years into this pandemic. Between helping others where I could, and bringing back all our staff, plus more, we're gearing up to be better than ever. My ears are raw from buds, my eyes will need surgery because of the Zoom devil, and the pandemic pounds are bastards.

My pants still don't fit, but now that I've navigated through the gale force winds of this small nightmare and have tied the boat back at the wharf for another trip, it's me time.

At least for a little while.

24

—

TRADE UP

Anyone who's watched even a single episode of home-reno reality TV will recognize one particular scene. There's an issue, some doozy of an issue—a supporting wall, say, in exactly the wrong place to allow the homeowner's dream to become a reality— that in an ordinary world is going to cost ten thousand dollars to deal with. Lo and behold, with a snap of the fingers, the designer comes up with a solution. Voilà.

Problem solved. Everything gets done—just as the designer ordered.

On my home-reno show—yes, you heard that right, *my* show— it's not the designer who'll get the glory for finding a solution, but the tradesperson: the electrician who comes up with some brilliant rewiring plan; the plumber who finds a way in seemingly impossible conditions to reroute the pipes; the carpenter who transforms utility into beauty.

In other words, the honours go to the problem solvers and geniuses onsite who are often overlooked.

As we wrap up this story, I'm preparing for a summer in Yarmouth, shooting scenes for *Trading Up*, my new HGTV series. Do I really want to be on TV? Has this been a dream of mine? I wouldn't say so, no. But a few years back, I gave an off-the-cuff exuberant, passionate speech after receiving the Royal Bank of Canada's Momentum Award given out by that fantastic organization, Women of Influence. I began with two words: "Holy shit." Followed by four more: "Momentum Mandy has arrived." By the time I was done, less than two minutes later, I'd covered my fish-bait-catching Yarmouth childhood; leaving home as a teenager with a dirty hockey bag; building my business from scratch; signing my first four-million-dollar contract by the age of twenty-five; and how I came into this industry "because it needed the biggest goddamn kick in the ass you ever saw, and I was just the one to do it." I told that crowd I was building the people who were going to build "the next world we're going to live in. And I'll tell you what. Most of them are women."

Amid the dancing and mingling that followed, a television executive approached me and said, point blank, "Holy fuck. Why aren't you on TV? You need to be on TV. The world needs to see more of you."

I wasn't convinced. I wasn't convinced what she said was true, and I wasn't convinced TV was something I wanted to do. But quickly, the real opportunity before me became clear. Bringing the message about the importance of the trades, the respect we owe to tradespeople, and the need for more women in the trades to a TV audience was worthwhile. It was more than that: it was called for. And who better to broadcast that message than me, the Blue Collar CEO? We have an industry that's in dire need of a makeover, and I already know I'm the one to do it. So whether, deep down, I wanted to be on camera or not, I had to give this the Rennehan try.

By now, this far into my story, you know what that means, don't you? Nothing halfway.

If I was going to do this, I was going to do it right. I met with the head of creative at Corus Entertainment, who agreed with me that I wasn't a "formula." I wasn't somebody you could tuck in a box. We'd have to find a concept that fit who I was and what I brought to the table. I started interviewing production companies, drumming up ideas. Nobody knew what to do with me. I wasn't normal. I'm not your 140-pound Barbie doll. I'm in my forties, I'm established, I'm chubby, I'm already a millionaire. I'm gay. I'm extremely candid—what I call "respectfully uncensored."

But after months of tossing concepts back and forth—no, actually a couple of years (with a pandemic thrown in, don't forget)—none of which excited me, I started to grow weary of the whole idea. Maybe this wasn't for me. I was ready to give up. Then, out of the blue, the creative team sat down and came up with a concept based on what I do every day, which is to mentor young people. To use the oldest construction cliché ever, that was it: she'd hit the nail on the head. I thought, *Wow, we could cultivate something powerful from this.*

Entrepreneurship and the trades go hand in hand. That's a reality I'm always trying to get across to people, because there's a huge disconnect out there, and I happen to be the pilot project that went really right. I've swum every ocean and climbed every tree in the business. The team took the time to consider me and thoughtfully came up with this idea that was right under our noses. And over yet another year, we fleshed it out.

We landed on the name *Trading Up*. On the show, I will train apprentices across Canada and the United States, starting with three carefully chosen participants of different genders and backgrounds who want to train under the Blue Collar CEO. For the first season, they'll work on my own properties in my hometown of Yarmouth, Nova Scotia. It's a huge risk, even a sacrifice, to train apprentices on these properties. Mistakes will be made. Things are going to take longer than, in ideal circumstances, they should. But that's the commitment I've made.

There will be no trends in this show. No rules. Just stunning, functional, timeless design. It's going to be based on my years of experience and my ability to transform something respectfully. Two of the properties we'll tackle are turn-of-the-century homes. The other one's my old wood shop, which we're going to resurrect as luxury flats. I call these properties my old friends.

My main project lead for the show is a thirty-year-old Red Seal carpenter who's Indigenous and female. We've got Mini, my design and construction manager, on my other arm, who's mentored under me for the past eight or nine years (and she's not even thirty yet, for shit's sake). They're going to be resources for these apprentices, too. We'll be on the job site every day, with the apprentices learning skills on the spot. We're putting them to work, holding them accountable for budgets, design, timelines—throwing them right in.

I've always believed that a show on TV could be inspirational, motivational, ethical, and funny as hell—and also have philanthropy at its core. When I watch TV there might be one or two of those things at play, but I believe, with *Trading Up*, we could check off every one of those boxes. This concept is groundbreaking. There has never been a show that paid tribute to the essentials of the trades industry. No show ever highlighted the trade professionals who actually execute those renos that have homeowners salivating and squirming with envy. No show ever gave due to the uncle, the brother, the dad who could do everything, fix anything. Everybody remembered him only as a "handyman"—or as a drunk. On *Trading Up*, the solutions will come through collaboration with the tradespeople onsite—the meat behind the potatoes!—as they do in real life.

These are the people with whom I've built my business. They're the mind and muscle, the skill, and the heart behind our infrastructure, our homes, and our way of life.

Without them, none of it comes to light.

ACKNOWLEDGEMENTS

Pam Mood, a.k.a. Momma, thank you for your genius wit, conviction, and love—and for getting my mind on paper.

To Janice, cheers to that morning you heard me on CBC Radio, knew I had more to say, and refused to quit till you tracked me down.

And thanks to Anita for your incessant late-night questions about luxury wood flooring, lobster fishing, and my love life.

To the rest of the team at HarperCollins, I owe you all a serious night out at the pub.

And to the love of my life, Lauren a.k.a. Annie: thank you for not trading me in for a new Bear and for tolerating my life. (I am a pain in the ass, but worth it.)

Thank you to my family for never questioning who or what I am long enough for it to matter. That non-judgment has paid off for all of us.